Midnight Snacks

150
EASY AND
ENTICING
ALTERNATIVES
TO STANDING
BY THE FREEZER
EATING ICE CREAM
FROM THE CARTON

MICHAEL J. ROSEN
SHARON REISS

BROADWAY BOOKS

NEW YORK

Midnight Snacks

Broadway Books titles may be purchased for business or promotional use or for special sales. For information, please write to: Special Markets Department, Random House, Inc., 1540 Broadway, New York, NY 10036.

PRINTED IN THE UNITED STATES OF AMERICA

BROADWAY BOOKS and its logo, a letter B bisected on the diagonal, are trademarks of Broadway Books, a division of Random House, Inc.

Visit our website at www.broadwaybooks.com

Book design by Pei Loi Koay
Illustrated by Michael J. Rosen

Library of Congress Cataloging-in-Publication Data
Rosen, Michael J., 1954–
Midnight snacks: 150 easy and enticing alternatives to standing by the freezer eating ice cream with a spoon / Michael J. Rosen, Sharon Reiss.—1st ed.
p.   cm.
Includes index.
1. Snack foods.   I. Reiss, Sharon.   II. Title.
TX740 .R593   2002
641.5'3—dc21

2002072051

FIRST EDITION

ISBN 0-7679-1104-0

10   9   8   7   6   5   4   3   2   1

For our circle of dear friends
who stay up snacking with us

Contents

INTRODUCTION   **x**

10:15 PM   PAST YOUR BEDTIME REPAST   **xii**

10:30 PM   COMFORT COOKING   **10**

10:45 PM   SLUMBER PARTY TIME   **20**

11:00 PM   AFTER AFTER-DINNER TREATS   **28**

11:15 PM   LAST BITES   **36**

11:30 PM   FIRESIDE FODDER   **46**

11:45 PM   NIGHTCAPPING   **58**

12:00 AM   THE BEWITCHING HOUR   **74**

12:15 AM   CRUNCHES BEFORE BED   **84**

12:30 AM   TOO DARNED HOT   **94**

12:45 AM   CRUMBS IN BED   **108**

1:00 AM   SPA NIGHT   **118**

1:15 AM   UNDER THE COVERS   **130**

1:30 AM   TOASTWICHES   **138**

1:45 AM   SKINNY DIPS & OTHER RAREBITS   **146**

2:00 AM   LOVE TRIANGLES   **156**

2:30 AM   LATE-NIGHT REHAB   **166**

5:30 AM   FIRST SHIFT FOODS   **176**

5:45 AM   DAWN'S EARLY LIGHT   **184**

INDEX   **192**

Midnight Snacks

Introduction

Midnight snacks—those furtive, indulgent, comforting, reviving, hasty meals—everyone partakes in them, few share them, and no one discusses them, let alone reads a cookbook about them—until now. Here, at last, is a celebration of the delicacies and comfort foods, the nibbly bits and noshes, that are cooked and often eaten in the dim glow of the microwave's green numerals.

When we began speaking with friends and chefs about a collection of offerings for midnight fare, we found that even folks renowned for their formidable fixings admitted to pretty ordinary fare. Spooning ice cream out of the carton in a haze of freezer condensation was the number-one guilty pleasure. Reheating leftovers tied with microwave popcorn for second place. We heard about impromptu Rice Krispies Treats made by stirring puffed rice into a mug of Marshmallow Fluff (an ingredient that's dubious in broad daylight); banana-nut cake eaten from the freezer in thin slices; bread-and-butter pickles sandwiched around cheese singles meant for the kids' lunches; ice-cream floats; celery sticks packed with cream cheese; graham crackers slathered with peanut butter and banana slices—such a paucity for such a profound need!

So we rose to the all-night occasion and turned up, fine-tuned, and forged anew an entire repertoire of awesome options for every species of night owl. We hoped to calibrate each chapter to the fickle waxings and wanings, prompts and petitions the body and soul make throughout the night. Therefore, we allowed the idea of "midnight snacking" to begin shortly after dinner and to conclude just before dawn's early light. So whether you're seeking an after after-dinner sweet, a bedtime bite when you let out the dog, a refrigerator raid during a commercial, a bowl of something to snack on while watching movies in bed, a taunting temptation for your new love, or crunchy bits to placate the midnight munchies—you'll find a sampling of manageable, marvelous edibles appropriate to the occasion and the hour.

Indeed, we jettisoned the usual cookbook chapters (appetizers, salads, soups, etc.) and arranged *Midnight Snacks* by hours of the night, beginning at 10:15 P.M. and, moving by quarter hours, ending at 5:45 A.M. Admittedly, we started getting pretty tired around 2:30, as we were reinventing hangover cures and insomnia teas, so we dozed off until 5:30, when we attempted to rise and shine and scrounge up some first-shift foods for breakfast.

Though we made a few exceptions, the demands of nocturnal cuisine were clear: Create dishes that require little forethought and minimal preparation; find dishes that respond to the impulsive craving or the impatient pang of hunger. That means the majority of recipes here take less than fifteen minutes, and many take less than five. We did allow that a couple of chapters could include dishes to share—tidbits to offer a bedmate, appetizers to serve to another couple you've invited over for a nightcap—but most of the dishes are designed to serve the needs of solo dining.

We also vowed to uphold a certain moderation: no worrying about protein/carbohydrate ratios, no delicate suspensions of egg yolks and oil, no sifting of powdered sugar through doily templates. It's time for bed, not bedlam. True, every now and then we do urge you to stock something in your freezer or pantry, just to make raiding the refrigerator more lucrative, but for the most part these dishes should be easy to concoct in any kitchen where something more than phone calls for carryout food is made.

What more is there to know other than the comforting thought that, in the wee hours of the night, alone, famished, and guilt-ridden in your darkened kitchen, you're in good company? And that now you have some 150 swell suggestions of what to cook. Who knew that the chiming of midnight was a dinner bell?

Past Your Bedtime Repast

Here are a few bites before bed, a few easy, comfortable, fix-in-a-jiffy dishes. Childhood favorites. Foods from when you still had a bedtime and someone to enforce it.

Here are foods reminiscent of Sharon's childhood favorite: a thin slice of chocolate cake floating like an island in a sea of milk. Something like what our friend Lizzie's British nanny offered before reading bedtime stories: "hundreds and thousands" sandwiches, little triangles of crust-free white bread, buttered and then encrusted with nonpareils (what the British call "hundreds and thousands").

The dishes offered here are little treats to nibble on while you're finally getting around to reading the day's mail . . . finally getting *your* chance—now that the kids, tucked in bed, have freed up the computer—to answer yesterday's e-mail . . . or finally watching the one grown-up video you sneaked into the six (already a day overdue) you rented for the kids.

A little something to serve when your daughter is having her newest, bestest friend sleep over for the night . . . or when half of your son's scouting troop is sleeping in the backyard tent (at least until the flashlight batteries dim and they decide to bivouac indoors).

Part reward, part refreshment, part relaxer, these dishes are for the kids to eat before you switch off the night-light . . . or for nights you want to be that kid, staying up late just to watch your grown-up program that doesn't come on until ten-thirty.

A sampling of bedtime bites for sleeping tight.

When you still had a bedtime and someone to enforce it

Impromptu Pizza

**1 fresh flour tortilla
(consider using spinach or
sun-dried tomato varieties)**

1 tablespoon olive oil

4 thin tomato slices

4 fresh basil leaves

**4 ounces fresh mozzarella
cheese, sliced or shredded**

**1 tablespoon freshly grated
Parmesan cheese**

**Salt and freshly
ground pepper**

★

SERVES 1

Why does everything have to come in "pizza" flavor? Egg rolls. Bagels. Corn chips, potato chips, pretzels, pork rinds. What's wrong with just pizza being pizza? Certainly the concept of flat dough smothered with sauces and melted cheese has been remodeled and redecorated by every wood-burning-oven chef in America, to say nothing of the damage done by the cafeteria ladies in elementary schools who have to provide something that resembles pizza every Friday for lunch.

But the fact remains: late-night pizza has been a subsistence food for college students and first-apartment dwellers for fifty years. With our impromptu pizzas, you get to cut out the thirty-minute wait for the delivery guy.

★ ★ ★

★ Preheat the oven or toaster oven to 400°F.

★ Place the tortilla on a baking sheet and brush with the olive oil.

★ Arrange the remaining ingredients on the tortilla in the order listed and sprinkle with salt and pepper.

★ Place the pizza in the oven and bake for 12 to 15 minutes or until the cheese is bubbly and golden.

★ Cool the pizza slightly; you don't want that scalded little piece of skin on the roof of your mouth.

VARIATIONS

Scrutinize the contents of your refrigerator and apply these basic pizza-making principles:

★ Crust alternatives: English muffins, lavosh, pita bread, bagels, matzo, wedges of prepared pizza crust, toasted French bread pieces, halved focaccia, etc.

★ Topping possibilities: tomato sauce, a cheesy white sauce, pesto, sun-dried-tomato or olive pesto, smashed roasted garlic cloves, caramelized onions, grilled chicken slices, roasted red peppers, slices of various sausages, sautéed mushrooms, etc.

★ Something cheesy: mozzarella, provolone, goat cheese, ricotta, Parmesan, and many other cheeses that can behave in a supporting, rather than leading, role.

Here, too, are three favorite combinations:

★ Peeled Brie spread over the crust and topped with apple butter, walnuts, and blue cheese

★ Raspberry preserves, smoked turkey, and Swiss cheese

★ Goat cheese, roasted corn, and chopped fresh herbs

Mashed Potato Pancakes

1 cup mashed potatoes

1 egg

¼ cup freshly grated
Parmigiano-Reggiano cheese,
plus extra for serving

Salt and freshly
ground pepper

A grating of nutmeg

Dash of Tabasco sauce or
cayenne pepper, optional

Flour for dusting

2 to 3 tablespoons oil for
frying, as needed

★

SERVES 2

When we were growing up, mashed potatoes were frequently a part of dinner. Always made from boiled, then mashed, potatoes and thinned, as it were, with whole milk and butter, this creamy dish was everyone's favorite. The leftovers, if any, almost invariably disappeared before they could be served again, lightly fried on a griddle as a bedtime snack.

If you do not have leftover real mashed potatoes, we'll permit you to use instant mashed potatoes once, but only once. After that, you'll need to commit to the program.

★ ★ ★

★ Combine the potatoes, egg, cheese, salt, pepper, nutmeg, and Tabasco in a mixing bowl. Mix together and then shape the mixture into two cakes.

★ Dust both sides of the cakes with flour. Pour the oil into a heavy skillet over high heat. Slide in the pancakes and turn the heat down to medium-high. Brown the cakes on each side and serve with additional cheese.

Have a Cow

Whether you were the sort of kid who preferred a black cow (cola with vanilla ice cream) to a brown cow (root beer with vanilla ice cream), you surely remember your elixir of choice as the cure-all for childhood mood swings. It was the parents' bargaining tool, the reward for dutiful behavior, the consolation prize for having to come inside on a night that was filled with lightning bugs when older kids got to stay out past dark. FYI: This simple marriage of ice cream and soda mollifies most adult disappointments as well.

★ ★ ★

2 small scoops
vanilla ice cream

8 ounces root beer
or cola

★

SERVES 1

- ★ Place the ice cream scoops in a tall glass.
- ★ Pour half of the soda over the ice cream and allow the carbonation to settle. Alternatively, you can do what you did as a child: overfill the glass and watch the foam run across the counter and the floor.
- ★ Fill with the remaining soda, insert a straw, and have your cow.

VARIATIONS

Orange Creamsicle: Scoop in the ice cream, but use a favorite fizzy orange soda instead of the cola or root beer. For an upscale version, ditch the soda pop and use ½ cup freshly squeezed orange juice and 1 cup sparkling water.

Cherry Cola: Replace the vanilla ice cream with cherry ice cream, and use cola rather than root beer. (You could make a cherry/root beer hybrid, no doubt, or any other concoction—grape soda with fudge ripple or red pop with mint-chocolate chip—but these rogue pairings are undertaken at your own risk.)

Popover Pancakes

½ cup all-purpose flour

½ cup milk

2 eggs

1 tablespoon unsalted butter

Juice of ½ lemon, strained

1 tablespoon
confectioners' sugar

Dollops of whipped cream,
sliced fresh berries, a favorite
jam, or butter and maple
syrup, optional

★

SERVES 2

This airy, oven-baked popover-of-a-pancake is ambidextrous, turning sweet or savory according to your needs and whims. More likely found on the brunching menu, this rise-and-shine standard is equally satisfying on a cold winter night in front of the fire or the television. Some evening try it with freshly grated Parmesan cheese, salt, and pepper. If you then decide that sweet just can't be beat, you can always bake another pancake and flood it with syrup . . . for dessert.

★ ★ ★

★ Preheat the oven to 425°F.

★ Combine the flour, milk, and eggs in a mixing bowl. Whisk to-gether, leaving the batter slightly lumpy.

★ Heat the butter in an 8-inch nonstick skillet with an ovenproof handle (or use an 8-inch pie plate).

★ Add the batter to the hot pan and bake for 17 to 20 minutes, or until the pancake is puffy and golden brown. Remove it from the oven and sprinkle the crusty surface with lemon juice and confection-ers' sugar. Serve warm, with whipped cream, berries, jam, or butter and maple syrup, if desired.

NOTE: You can also make 4 individual portions using a muffin pan. Place the pan in a hot oven for several minutes, mist the pan with cooking spray, and add bits of butter to 4 cups. Pour the batter into these cups and pour a small amount of water into the empty cups to keep the pan heating evenly.

VARIATION

For the more savory version, eliminate the lemon juice and confectioners' sugar. To the batter, add ½ teaspoon salt, ½ teaspoon freshly ground pepper, and 2 tablespoons freshly grated Parmesan cheese. Bake the popover as directed, sprinkling the finished dish with 1 additional tablespoon of the cheese.

Buckeye Bars

2 cups smooth peanut butter

1 cup puffed rice cereal (such as Rice Krispies), optional

2½ cups confectioners' sugar

1½ cups graham cracker crumbs (8 whole graham crackers)

½ cup packed light brown sugar

½ cup unsalted butter, melted

2 cups semisweet chocolate chips or 8 ounces semisweet chocolate, chopped

1 tablespoon vegetable shortening

★

MAKES 3 TO 4 DOZEN PIECES

Not surprisingly, 80 percent of the peanut butter in the United States is slathered on sandwiches. Ten percent is mixed into cookies. As for the remaining 10 percent, we're guessing it's consumed straight from the jar late at night. The average citizen manages close to four pounds of the spread each year.

This recipe, named for Ohio's state tree, which produces glossy chocolate-colored nuts with one peanut-colored spot, is a pure union of peanut butter and chocolate. Since these bars require no baking and almost no time to assemble, you'll no longer have any excuse for standing at the cupboard swabbing the peanut butter jar with your index finger.

★ ★ ★

★ Line a 10 x 15-inch pan with aluminum foil or parchment paper.

★ Combine the peanut butter, optional rice cereal, confectioners' sugar, graham cracker crumbs, brown sugar, and melted butter in a large mixing bowl and stir them together. Press the mixture into the prepared pan.

★ Melt the chocolate and shortening in a double boiler or in the microwave oven set on low.

★ Spread the melted chocolate mixture evenly over the peanut butter mixture. Refrigerate until firm. Cut the mixture into hefty 2-inch squares or use a cookie cutter to cut the mixture into interesting shapes.

"Gram" does not refer to one of our beloved grandmothers. No, this recipe calls for graham crackers and uses a quick-and-not-so-dirty process no doting grandmother would ever condone. But these crunchy and casual treats are guaranteed to appeal to any kid— even the ones who grew up to read cookbooks.

- ★ Preheat the oven to 325°F.
- ★ Line a small baking sheet with aluminum foil. Arrange the crackers flat, edges touching, in a single layer.
- ★ In a small saucepan, melt the butter, add the brown sugar, and stir until the sugar dissolves.
- ★ Pour the mixture over the crackers, sprinkle with the nuts, and bake for 10 minutes.
- ★ Make the kids wait until the crackers are completely cool, then break the treats into crispy chunks.

**3 whole graham crackers
(6 "squares")**

¼ cup unsalted butter

**¼ cup packed dark
brown sugar**

**¼ cup almond slivers
or chopped pecans**

★

MAKES 6 SQUARES

10:30 PM

Comfort
Cooking

Something comforting to coddle if molly-coddling can be food

When you're under the weather and under the covers and, invariably, under the gun on a deadline you inherited from someone who was let go and you were only helping and look where it got you: Nothing seems worth eating . . . especially if you have to prepare it. If only someone else could see that you wouldn't dream of bothering them, but would they really mind? It's tea you need, tea and sympathy . . . and something to dunk in the tea . . . and maybe a little something just to keep your stomach from growling.

Yes, maybe you could eat just the *right* something . . . nothing too spicy or too sweet. Something bland to counter the blahs, something comforting to coddle your grousy mood, something like nursery food: that food you want when you want your mommy. Yes, it's been decades since you thought that, and Mommy's not here, but the food can be. You can trundle over to the kitchen and make it . . . yes, you can.

Our two favorites were elbow macaroni smothered with cottage cheese and maybe butter. Pale mixed with pale for a kid feeling pale. Or leftover rice with warm milk and raisins.

If mollycoddling can be a food, these would be its incarnations: dishes that tap into the well-being center of the brain, that primitive part deep in the medulla oblongata or wherever it is you store the scent of opening a Tinker Toy canister or the primal taste of tapioca pudding.

Here are soothers and restoratives, spirit lifters and appetite cajolers—custom-ordered for the bellyaching, the bedridden, the bedraggled, or those who're feeling that the day got the better of them.

Cures-What-Ails-Ya Soup

1 cup chicken stock (fresh,
frozen, or canned)

1 tablespoon grated
fresh ginger

Juice of 1 juicy lime

2 teaspoons soy sauce
(we prefer low-sodium)

1 tablespoon scallion slivers
(whole scallions cut on
an angle)

1 small bundle of rice noodles
(softened by soaking in
boiling water for 2 to 3
minutes, then snipped into
3-inch pieces—save half for
tomorrow) or
½ cup cooked rice, reheated

Chopped fresh cilantro,
optional

★

SERVES 1

Some philosopher—was it Nietzsche?—said something like joy joins hands in a circle with others, while misery holds its hands in its lap. How does this translate into culinary terms? Well, the basic idea is you want to be feeling better and join in the smorgasbord of life again, but for now all you can think of is sitting up and taking soup all by your lonesome. Okay, so here's that soup. It's a heartwarming heal-all certain to make you feel better.

★ ★ ★

★ Combine the stock, ginger, lime juice, and soy sauce in a microwave-safe bowl or mug. Cover and microwave on high for 2 minutes. Remove and allow the mixture to steep for 5 minutes before straining.

★ Add the scallions and the noodles or rice to the strained soup. Reheat until the soup is piping hot again.

★ Add the cilantro or one of the other options below.

OPTIONS

Depending on your level of hunger, add whatever appeals at the moment:

★ Strips of cooked chicken or turkey, or cubes of tofu

★ Thinly julienned raw vegetables or leftover cooked vegetables

★ Torn or chopped leaves of salad lettuces or greens—watercress, spinach, arugula, kale, etc.

★ Sprouts, fresh herbs, mushroom slices, etc.

Get-Well-Sooner Pudding

For scratchy throat, winter blahs, allover achiness: this pudding is just what the doctor ordered. (Actually, the doctor might have prescribed a lovely couple of weeks in Aruba or one of those Greek islands you can't remember how to pronounce, but fat chance of that.)

Still, there's no reason not to add this creamy and hot rice pudding to your recovery tactics. It also doubles as a down-home dessert for all-better days.

★ ★ ★

- ★ Warm the milk in a small saucepan.
- ★ Add the cooked rice, your choice of dried fruits, and stir over low heat until the pudding is thickened and piping hot.
- ★ Remove the pudding from the heat and stir in the vanilla extract. Divide the pudding between two bowls.
- ★ Add half the butter to each pudding and sprinkle with a generous spoonful of cinnamon sugar and/or a dusting of freshly grated nutmeg.

⅔ cup whole milk

1 cup cooked white rice

Assorted dried fruits, such as currants, blueberries, or cherries, optional

½ teaspoon vanilla extract

1 tablespoon unsalted butter

Cinnamon sugar and/or freshly grated nutmeg

★

SERVES 2

Rice Water Tonic

You can brew a natural tonic for settling upset stomachs by boiling 1 cup of uncooked rice in 3 cups of water for 10 minutes. Strain off the starchy liquid and chill it. Drink up and let nature take its course. (Of course, rice water doesn't sound delicious. We're talking relief here, not refreshment.)

Don't-Be-So-Stuffy Soup

Leftover stuffing
(see Note that follows)

Milk

★

SERVES 1

OPTIONAL ADDITIONS

Salt and freshly
ground pepper

Butter

Hot sauce

Sour cream

Pesto

Ramen noodles,
broken into bits

Greens, chopped

First, a bedtime story. A friend urged us to join a cooking class at a local country club. She wanted us to meet the new chef, and we were only too glad to spend a winter weekend morning adding new soups to our repertoire. Chef Antoine (previous to this posh hire, Tony) divided us apprentices into teams so that we might conquer eight different soups, from the lowly lentil and bean to the rarified clarified consommé. We sipped wine (already an established part of our repertoire). We learned that dried beans, if frozen overnight, create less gastrointestinal distress (now this was news to us). We roasted chicken bones for brown stock, pounded lobster shells for bisques, hovered over a browning roux with filé powder for gumbo. Two hours later, we sampled the eight soups with various breads and more of the same wine.

Yet the day's real revelation came not from planned culinary coaching but from one of the attendees, the wife of a prominent lawyer, who touted her own invention: leftovers soup. "Basically," she explained, "I toss whatever leftovers I have right into the blender and add enough skim milk to keep the blades whirring." Then heat and eat.

And while she allowed that she invents a new soup with each week's leftovers (hinting that meats are best left out of the process and added, if at all, after the blending), her all-time favorite is stuffing soup, something that she doesn't relegate to Thanksgiving alone.

Now this fascinated everyone at our table as we considered the concept of stuffing soup: some sort of bread, celery, onions, stock, herbs, mushrooms or giblets, some liquid base. Hey, weren't these among the most typical soup ingredients, just conveniently "premeasured" and "precooked"? Did this not sing out "midnight snack"?

Here's our own version, which we call "Don't-Be-So-Stuffy Soup," just to keep us all open to late-night possibilities. It's little more than permission to peek inside your own fridge for such overlooked soup candidates as ratatouille, mashed potatoes, and cooked vegetables. Or how about baked beans and coleslaw and shredded cheese for a makeshift Alsatian cabbage soup, which is essentially white beans, Gruyère, ham stock, carrot, onions, celery, and milk?

The possibilities are dizzying.

- Find a bowl that's about the size of your hunger. Fill half the bowl with stuffing, then empty this into the blender jar. Fill half the bowl with milk and pour into the blender.
- Purée to your heart's content. Try a few buttons on the blender; they all work the same wonder.
- Microwave or heat on top of the stove until the soup is hot.
- A sample taste might suggest some small enhancement besides salt or pepper: a pat of butter or a squirt of hot sauce, a swirl of sour cream or pesto, a sprinkling of crispy ramen noodles or chopped-up greens.

NOTE: If your stuffing involves ingredients whose ground texture might not be appreciated in a creamy soup—say, apricots and oysters, or sausages and pecans—you might want to abandon the soup idea and just heat 'n' eat the stuffing. Our preferred method: slice a wedge in half and fry each half in a skillet with a little butter to renew that crispy crust.

Milky Way

Many of our recipes call for milk. Unless we specify otherwise, you should feel free to consult your doctor or your conscience and either slide up or down the fat scale by choosing whole, 2%, skim, half-and-half, whipping cream, or any sort of soy or rice milk. Yogurt thinned with water or milk often works perfectly in recipes that don't require heating. Or use what's stocked in your fridge or pantry.

Consider stocking a few cans of evaporated milk (also available in low-fat versions) and boxed cartons of milk and soy milk in your cupboard.

Milk Toast

2 slices of buttercrust bread

2 teaspoons unsalted butter

**1 tablespoon cinnamon sugar
(that's just sugar with some
cinnamon in it)**

**1 cup milk, steaming (use the
microwave or a saucepan)**

★

SERVES 1

Maybe this bit of nursery food will evoke early memories of sleepy time or cuddling, of being dandled on Grandma's knees or pounding the highchair tray with a sippy cup. In any case, the primal flavors of milk, cinnamon, sugar, and toast are the stuff that comfort's made of.

So if you're feeling peaked, milk toast is perfect: it takes all of three minutes to prepare, there's nothing to clean up, and you'll be back in bed before the cat has stolen your place on the pillow.

★ ★ ★

★ Toast slices of bread. Go on, you're up to it.

★ Spread butter on the toast and sprinkle with the cinnamon sugar.

★ Place the toast in a bowl and pour the steaming milk over it. Let it soak for 30 seconds while you settle back in bed. Take a spoonful. Close your eyes. Remember a lullaby your granny used to sing to you. There, there. All better now?

Congee

Soup—it's not just for breakfast anymore. This thin rice porridge is a familiar breakfast dish and curative in areas of Japan, India, China (where it is called jook), and the region once known as Persia. The word congee comes from the Indian kanji, which means boilings. Now that we have that settled, on to settling the stomach: congee is not only a gentle breakfast boost but also a soothing remedy for those times when your appetite has flagged or your stomach has called in sick. There's hardly any dish that's easier on the system.

Traditionally, this soup takes several hours to cook, but we've worked in a bit of time-lapse cookery, enabling you to create this soup in 30 minutes.

Finally, let's be frank: what's a euphemism for bland? Let's say agreeable. So unless you're feeling very sickly, consider enlivening this agreeable potage with one or another of the oddments listed below.

- ★ Rinse the rice and combine it with the water, chicken stock, salt, and oil in a medium saucepan. Bring to a boil and reduce the heat to a simmer, cooking uncovered.
- ★ After about 15 minutes of cooking, smoosh the rice with a potato masher for 1 minute so that some of the rice breaks and the broth turns cloudy.
- ★ Add the cooked meat, if you're going that route, and simmer for 10 to 15 more minutes. Mash the congee once more.
- ★ The soup should be thin and creamy. Ladle into bowls and serve with any of the oddments you choose.

½ cup white rice

4 cups bottled water (just to be purifying; tap water will work as well)

1 cup chicken stock

1 teaspoon salt (less if your stock is salted)

1 teaspoon vegetable oil

½ cup shredded cooked chicken, turkey, beef, or pork, optional

★

SERVES 2

ODDMENTS

1 teaspoon chopped fresh ginger

Shredded lettuce

1 scallion, finely chopped, green part included

Splash of soy sauce

Splash of sesame oil

Pinch of freshly ground pepper

Congestion Buster

Juice of 1 lemon

1 tablespoon maple syrup

⅛ teaspoon cayenne pepper

1 cup boiling water

★

SERVES 1

We know, nothing seems to help. Zinc lozenges leave your mouth feeling as if you've been sucking on, well, zinc. You've had so much tea you feel like a reused teabag yourself.

Now, the FDA has not verified this claim, of course, but this tonic seems to relieve the upper respiratory congestion from colds, flu, bronchitis, and asthma. Again, our lawyers advise us to reiterate: this is not a cure, but you will feel the heat as it soothes. Our lawyers say that it's also good for relieving the strain of constantly dispensing advice.

★ Combine the lemon juice, maple syrup, and cayenne in a large coffee mug.

★ Add the water and stir. Cover with a saucer or plastic wrap for 1 minute before sipping very slowly.

Gingery Lemon Infusion

Not that you need an extra reason to brew a cup of this, but ginger happens to be touted as a remedy for everything from lumbago to coughing, from diarrhea to fever, from vomiting to stomach pain. Plus, it's frequently dispensed as a cure for motion sickness and as an aphrodisiac. How a little piece of ginger knows which of its talents you require is just one of its mysteries.

The following infusion is a general feel-better brew. Iced, it also works as a sort of summery refresco.

⋆ ★ ⋆

- ★ Combine all the ingredients in a glass measuring cup or a small stainless-steel bowl. Cover with plastic wrap and steep for 10 minutes.
- ★ Strain into teacups and reheat in the microwave oven until hot. If you'd prefer to serve this cold, pour the infusion over cracked ice.

2 cups boiling water

½ cup fresh lemon juice

2 tablespoons honey

One 3-inch piece fresh ginger, coarsely chopped (no need to peel, just wash)

★

SERVES 2

10:45 PM

Slumber Party Time

We all scream for ice cream, right? It's just that your stomach—if not the kids themselves—is screaming, "I don't want that flavor," referring to the last bit of butter-pecan left over from Grandma's birthday. (It's her favorite, not yours.)

It is true: Wherever in the world there are freezers, there are frozen desserts and children who'd be happy, and probably healthy, eating nothing but those freezer treats. As for adults, according to our survey, the most widespread midnight-snacking activity is standing in the fog of the freezer, dipping into a carton of ice cream, thinking maybe just a tablespoon or two. We put the carton back. We rinse the spoon. We start to turn out the light and think, That could hardly be called a snack, so we open the freezer again and take a big spoonful, licking it like a small cone. And now look, there's not even enough left in the carton for anyone else to eat . . . and we can't leave an empty carton in the freezer. Ah, the story of our lives.

Rather than relinquish this all-important nighttime ritual to the iffy prospects of the freezer, we offer you the chance for sudden sorbets, instantaneous ice creams, and a few methods of bypassing the age-old vanilla standby or the frostbitten orange sherbet and creating an ice-cream parlor of fresh flavors and appealing treats.

What follows are freezer pleazers: dishes as fun to share as to hoard for yourself . . . fruited frappés to fix up when you're hosting the slumber party . . . a homemade ice-cream sandwich to offer up to your nieces and nephews when they've come for a weekend visit so they'll think you're as sweet as the treats you're serving. And even a couple of sauces to prove that you're no soda jerk.

Chopped Ice Cream

The new trend in swanky ice-cream shops is to stock slightly fewer than thirty-one ice creams but to boast an infinite number of flavors by offering an enormous array of chips, crumbs, candies, squirts, and goobers to tailor-make nearly any ice-cream flavor out of one of the basics, such as vanilla or chocolate. It's like custom-tinting cans of neutral paint at the hardware store. You simply announce your all-time favorite or your whim of the moment, and the soda jerk slaps some ice cream on a marble board and, Japanese–steak-house style, chops and slices the various ingredients necessary to create your individual treat.

This method can be replicated at home, even if the spectrum of flavor possibilities is a bit narrower. Here is the process below; simply dream up the ingredients that make your taste buds scream for more.

★ ★ ★

★ Place a portion of ice cream on a cutting board or, better yet, on a small marble slab that you can keep in the freezer for occasions like this. Basic flavors like vanilla or chocolate ice cream or orange or lemon sherbet are the most versatile.

★ Using a pastry scraper or large chef's knife, chop the ice cream into bits and then sprinkle or squirt whatever ingredients you desire onto the ice cream. Perhaps these will inspire you: crushed graham crackers, biscotti, or cookies; crumbled cake or ladyfingers; candied walnuts, coconut patties, cinnamon red hots; squirts of fruit or chocolate sauces or syrups; candied ginger, citrus peel, or chocolate chunks; sliced fresh fruit; assorted penny candies, malted milk balls, or soft Halloween candy; instant coffee granules; a splash of brandy or fruit liqueur.

★ Scrape, chop, smoosh, and fold the ice cream to incorporate the goodies. You have a couple minutes to work with it before you end up making ice-cream soup.

★ Use the pastry scraper to shape and scoop up your new flavor and place it in a bowl or a cone.

VARIATIONS

Here are some best-loved combinations:

★ Orange or raspberry sherbet with bittersweet chocolate pieces

★ Vanilla ice cream with chocolate bits, cake crumbs drizzled with brandy, and instant coffee granules (a mock tiramisu)

★ Chocolate ice cream with smashed peppermint patties

★ Vanilla and chocolate ice cream with bits of ready-to-bake cookie dough from the fridge

★ Vanilla ice cream with candied lime peel and crushed graham crackers (a key lime pie version)

★ For a decadent evening: the entire contents of the Godiva chocolates boxes your in-laws sent you for Valentine's Day, chopped up

★ For a sublime version, suitable for the finish of a casual dinner party: fresh basil leaves, freshly cracked black pepper, and a scraping of a vanilla bean's tiny seeds

Homemade Ice-Cream Sandwiches

Not that we resist those ice-cream sandwiches dispensed from vending machines, swimming pool snack bars, and bell-dinging trucks, but making homemade versions of this treat is something even kids can manage. (It's just impossible to re-create the sodden, dry, pliable, syrupy, ineluctable texture those wrapped confections achieve.)

Your favorite ice cream can be pressed between any number of genuinely crispy or spongy or wafery layers. You can deploy cookies purchased from your local bakery or a gourmet cookie company. If there's an Italian bakery in your neck of the woods, pick up some fresh pizzelle. Vanilla or chocolate pound cake slices are yummy. Hell, your great-aunt's rugalach can only be improved with ice cream pinched between a pair. And don't forgo a childhood favorite: leftover waffles from Sunday breakfast.

Snappy Ice-Cream Sandwiches

4 small scoops vanilla, cinnamon, or caramel ice cream

8 soft gingersnap cookies (see recipe on page 26, or use a store-bought variety)

Chopped nuts, optional

★

MAKES 4 ICE-CREAM SANDWICHES

★ Sandwich each scoop of ice cream between two cookies. Press gently to flatten the ice cream without breaking the cookies.

★ Once all four sandwiches are assembled, roll their edges in the nuts, if desired. Refreeze for 10 to 15 minutes. Any sandwiches that aren't to be eaten right away should be wrapped in a double layer of waxed paper.

VARIATIONS

★ Press chocolate-covered butter cookies around vanilla or coffee ice cream.

★ Slice a thick brownie into two thin layers and slide a wedge of ice cream between them.

★ Fill two macadamia-nut cookies with lime sorbet, and think Hawaiian.

★ Kids will love a parade of large animal crackers (match the elephant with elephant, bear with bear, etc.) with rainbow sherbet between the pairs.

Ice-Cream Sandwich Waffles

★ Spread the ice cream over one waffle half and cover it with the other half.

★ Refreeze or drizzle with sauce. Spurt with whipped cream if you have some, then serve.

**1 slab ice cream,
your choice of flavor**

**1 homemade or store-bought
waffle, toasted and halved**

**¼ cup ice-cream fruit sauce,
optional (see sidebar)**

Whipped cream, optional

★

SERVES 1

Quick Fruit Sauce

An easy fruit sauce can be stewed up in minutes using any jam, jelly, or preserves you have on hand. The idea is simply to warm and thin the condensed fruit. Stir a bit of water into a few tablespoons of preserves and microwave on medium for a few seconds. Stir and microwave again as necessary to create the desired syrupy consistency. A tablespoon of brandy or a fruit-flavored liqueur adds some pizzazz.

Snappy Ginger Snaps

4 tablespoons unsalted butter

½ cup molasses

1 teaspoon baking soda

1¼ cups all-purpose flour

1 tablespoon chopped
crystallized ginger, optional

1 tablespoon ground ginger

½ teaspoon dry mustard

½ cup packed brown sugar

★

MAKES 15 TO 18 COOKIES

Don't relegate these cookies to the outsides of ice-cream sandwiches alone. Of course, they are delicious dunked in milk, just as you remember from elementary school, but you must also try them with fruit and blue cheese. They're terrific crumbled in the trifles on page 81. You might even try doubling the ginger (or adding a tablespoon of grated fresh ginger) as well, for a cookie that possesses the sweet, hot bite you know from the pickled ginger that's served with sushi.

★ ★ ★

★ Preheat the oven to 350°F.

★ Melt the butter with the molasses in a saucepan over low heat, or in the microwave set on low. Add the baking soda to the melted mixture; expect a bit of fizz. Set aside.

★ Mix together the flour, gingers, mustard, and brown sugar in a large mixing bowl. Add the butter mixture and stir to combine.

★ Line baking sheets with parchment paper or silicone baking liners and drop tablespoon-size mounds of dough onto the sheets 1 inch apart.

★ Bake for 12 to 15 minutes or until firm. Cool on racks.

Marshmallow Sauce

Just in case some small child suddenly asks you where marshmallows come from and how these odd little puffs got their name, here's what you say: Back in ancient Egypt, long before jelly beans and Pez were invented, the Pharaoh's children wanted something to roast and squeeze between graham crackers with chocolate bars. So some smart fellow created a honey-based candy flavored, as well as thickened, with the sap from the marsh mallow plant's roots. (That's Althea officinalis, *in case the child knows Latin.) Marsh mallow grows in marshes (surprise!). It even grows on stream banks throughout the eastern half of the United States, which is something to know in case the convenience store is closed and you're out of Marshmallow Fluff. For the last 150 years, gelatin has replaced the sap; the name could have been changed to "gelatin puffs with gum arabic and corn syrup" or something like that, but there's something quaint about the old version.*

Drizzle this sticky, sweet sauce over an ice-cream treat or anything else that needs a soupçon of excess.

★ ★ ★

2 cups mini marshmallows (or chop up some of the big ones)

3 tablespoons heavy cream

½ teaspoon vanilla extract

★

MAKES 2 CUPS

- ★ Place the marshmallows and heavy cream in a large glass or stainless-steel bowl. Pour an inch or so of water into a saucepan that's small enough to hold the bowl over, but not in, the water. (Yes, you *could* use your double-boiler.)
- ★ Bring the water to a simmer, stirring the marshmallow cream until it's smooth—3 to 5 minutes.
- ★ Remove from the heat and stir in the vanilla before ladling the sauce over ice cream.

After After–Dinner Treats

You're finished eating, snacking, entertaining, and puttering in the kitchen, and you have but one final longing: a single, lingering burst of exquisiteness . . . a chocolate. Somehow, nothing says "finis" like chocolate. (Moreover, nothing says "just one more" like chocolate, as well as "much too much.")

Not only does chocolate have a lot to say, but there's a lot to say about chocolate; lucky for us, most of it's been said. For instance, there's caffeine in chocolate, so we trust you not to consume any of the next few recipes if you know you'll be staring at the ceiling all night. Chocolate is not worth losing sleep over.

Superlative chocolate is as potent as cognac or truffles, evolving in subtle stages as the tongue and nose and palate all chime in, like the three blind men encountering an elephant, offering their unique perceptions.

Considering the hour, we wanted to temper a bit of chocolate's decadence in the sweets we're offering, but we refused to spare any of its exquisiteness. We abide by, and we feel you should as well, another Law of Culinary Physics: It makes no sense to indulge in anything less than the best. Keep a few bars of great bittersweet chocolate on hand so you won't be tempted by the junk in the kids' trick-or-treat sack.

From a brash, sensational chocolate-rimmed martini (admittedly, it doesn't clink when you raise a toast) to handmade mints for your pillow, from pistachio-studded white chocolate bark to bite-size chocolate ice-cream balls, we've set out a chocolateria of treats to lure the suspecting and the unsuspecting to the wiles of the cocoa bean. And what's more, we did it all without linking chocolate to phrases with words like *suicide* and *death.* (Attention pastry chefs: You're creating a dessert menu, not a coroner's report.)

a single lingering burst of exquisiteness

2 ounces bittersweet chocolate, grated or chopped

6 ounces ice-cold vodka or gin

2 ounces Cointreau

2 ounces dry vermouth

1 blood orange, quartered, optional

4 strips of orange zest (use a peeler and strip off a narrow curlicue of orange peel, removing any white pith), optional

★

SERVES 4

Now for something festive for a foursome. Something tempestuous for two. Something utterly inadvisable for one. With each sip of this martini, the lips' warmth melts a bit of the glass's chocolate rim. Yes, this is what it truly means to be a chocoholic.

Although the chocolate rims take less than a few minutes to create, you can prep them ahead of time and store the dipped glasses in the refrigerator until you're ready to sip.

★ ★ ★

★ Place the chocolate bits in a shallow plastic bowl at least 6 inches in diameter. Melt the chocolate in the microwave on a low setting for 30 seconds; stir and repeat for another 30 seconds. You can also melt the chocolate in a bowl over a pan of simmering water, hovering for 10 minutes as if you had nothing better to do.

★ Dip the rim of each martini glass ¼ inch deep into the pooled chocolate. Lift each glass straight up and hold it upside down over the chocolate until the rim has firmed up a bit. Then refrigerate the glasses while you mix the cocktail.

★ Pour the vodka, Cointreau, and vermouth into an ice-filled martini shaker and—what else?—shake it for several seconds. For an extra blush of color, squeeze a section of blood orange into the mix.

★ Divide the icy concoction among the chocolate-rimmed glasses and garnish with that optional twist of orange, if using.

Ice-Cream Bites in Chocolate Shells

These are an homage to those little ice-cream treats sold in movie theaters during our childhood. To fancy it up, we thought of naming the dish with the French for "ice-cream nubbins in a nun's habit"—but this dish is too straightforward for such an appellation. It's more of a stay-at-home version of vanilla ice cream dipped in a hardening chocolate coating at the local dairy freeze—but without the added paraffin or the risk of dripping all over your dad's leather car seats.

★ ★ ★

12 small scoops of your favorite ice cream

6 ounces bittersweet chocolate, chopped or grated

★

MAKES 12 PIECES

★ Cut twelve pieces of waxed paper on parchment paper into squares measuring 6 inches by 6 inches. Line a tray or plate with waxed paper.

★ Scoop the ice cream with the large end of a melon baller or use a small ice-cream scoop. Place the frozen balls on the waxed-paper-lined tray.

★ Freeze the tray with the ice cream for 10 minutes.

★ In a small plastic container, melt the chocolate in the microwave oven, using 10- to 15-second bursts and stirring between heating periods. Stop when there's just a bit of unmelted chocolate; the final stirring will finish the process. Allow the chocolate to cool for a few moments; it should be soupy but not hot.

★ Smear 1 tablespoon of the melted chocolate into a 4-inch circle in the center of a paper square. Plunk one knob of ice cream in the center of the chocolate and carefully lift each corner of the paper, enrobing the ice-cream ball safely inside the chocolate. Work quickly. You want the chocolate to remain warm enough to mold around the frozen bite.

★ Repeat the process for the other ice-cream balls, placing the finished balls on a baking sheet and refreezing for at least 10 minutes. To avoid a chocolate mess, work with only a few ice-cream balls at one time.

White Chocolate Bark

6 ounces white chocolate (a high-quality brand, such as Lindt, will make a real difference in taste), chopped

½ cup pistachios, toasted and chopped

½ cup golden raisins, chopped apricots, or dried cranberries

★

SERVES 2 TO 4

Some people consider white chocolate not to be chocolate at all, even though it boasts pure cocoa butter (and sugar and milk powder to distinguish it from suntan oil). But we're here to tell you that this subtle offspring of the cocoa bean is the consummate liaison for goodies of all sorts. Whether you call this a bark (so it's white; think birch trees) or a brittle or break it into bars, this treat may become a test of your willpower.

★ ★ ★

★ Line a jelly-roll pan with plastic wrap, pressing the bottom and sides to create a smooth surface.

★ Melt the chocolate in a plastic bowl in the microwave. Use the microwave's low setting for 15 to 20 seconds, stir, and then microwave for another 15 to 20 seconds. Continue heating and stirring until the chocolate has melted. Do not use high heat or leave the chocolate unattended; it can burn very quickly.

★ Stir the nuts and dried fruit into the melted chocolate and then spread the mixture in a thin layer in the prepared pan. Place in the freezer until the chocolate is brittle, about 10 minutes. Break into bite-size pieces and bits.

★ Fold crushed peppermint candies into the melted chocolate.

★ Replace the pistachios with peanuts, Brazil nuts, macadamia nuts, pecans, or walnuts. The golden raisins can be replaced with dried sour cherries, bits of candied orange peel, or chips of crystallized ginger.

★ For a crunchy texture, mix puffed rice cereal (such as Rice Krispies) into the melted chocolate.

★ If you're decidedly a milk- or a dark-chocolate person, you can use those rather than white chocolate in this bark.

Choco-Talk

It turns out that satisfying your chocolate craving can help your poor overworked heart. Cocoa beans have flavonoids!—those antioxidants that recondition your heart and circulatory system. A small dark-chocolate bar can have as much flavonoid power as six apples or a big pot of tea or seven bottles of white wine (but then the wine *does* have other advantages).

But before you commit to a cardiovascular program of gourmet chocolates, remember (as if you could forget!) that the candy also comes with an abundance of saturated fats and sugar.

As for white chocolate? It possesses none of the cocoa beans flavonoids. Another reason to dutifully eat your vegetables.

Chocolate Almonds

1 cup almonds

2 ounces high-quality
chocolate, grated

1 tablespoon high-quality
cocoa powder

2 tablespoons
confectioners' sugar

★

MAKES 1 CUP

A cup of almonds (especially after they're roasted and dusted with chocolate) is easy to devour in a single sitting, but we'd like to go on record urging you to savor them over a couple of nights, even as you're reasoning how they're chocablock with protein and cancer-fighting laetrile. Since these will keep in a sealed tin for a week or so, you have every reason to double or quadruple the recipe. They make swell hostess gifts, by the way, on the off-chance you actually know someone who refers to herself as a hostess.

★ ★ ★

★ Place the almonds in a dry skillet and toast them over medium-high heat for 5 minutes, shaking the pan frequently to keep the nuts from burning.

★ Remove the pan from the heat and add the grated chocolate to the nuts. Stir with a wooden spoon or with your fingers until the almonds are covered. (Be careful: the nuts will be hot.)

★ Spread the nuts on waxed paper and dust them with the cocoa powder.

★ Dust an additional sheet of waxed paper with the confectioners' sugar and toss the cocoa-covered nuts with the sugar until they're white.

★ Allow the nuts to cool slightly before eating. If you're feeling particularly impatient or sleepy, pop them in the freezer to chill quickly.

Frosted Chocolate Mint Leaves

These may be the lightest bedtime bites of all: a snip of cool mint with the slightest dabbing of chocolate. They're the soul of a peppermint patty, without its earthly body. Refreshing as they are to sample from the freezer, they can also moonlight as a subtle garnish for a bowl of raspberries or strawberries.

★ ★ ★

★ Lay a small sheet of parchment or waxed paper on a dinner plate.

★ Wash the mint leaves and pat dry with paper towels.

★ Carefully melt the chocolate in a heatproof dish over hot water or in the microwave on the lowest setting for up to 1 minute; check after 20 and then 40 seconds. When almost melted, stir the chocolate without further heat to complete the melting process.

★ Holding the leaves by their stems, press each of them into the melted chocolate, coating just the underside. Lift each leaf free and set it, chocolate side up, on the lined dinner plate.

★ Freeze the coated leaves for 5 minutes and then pluck each one from the frosty plate, savoring them in the fog of the open door.

10 fresh mint leaves with stems

1 ounce high-quality dark chocolate, chopped coarsely

★

MAKES 10 LEAVES

11:15 PM

Last Bites

One bite when you walk in from driving the babysitter home. One small reward for changing the burned-out lightbulb in your closet, which maybe could have waited for the weekend, but so could most anything and then what would the weekend be but one big chore—like workdays? One little something before you brush your teeth. Maybe a mint on the pillow. Hotels certainly think you deserve one, and they hardly know what kind of day you had. (But they do know you just paid a dollar twenty-five for a local call, ten dollars to use their Internet hook-up, and three dollars for a bottle of Sprite. You should get a free mint.)

In this chapter we consider the last bite of the night: a little nothing that's still a definite something. Something small enough so there's no angel/devil on your shoulders inveigling you to yield, resist, yield, resist, like two couples sincerely wrestling for the check that no one wants to pay anyway.

And if your household is anything like ours, since you're having one last bite before turning in you'll want to offer one to the puppy after her last round of the backyard before she monopolizes the covers, making you have to get out the afghan to cover your shoulders. And what about a little biscuit to get the kitty to cut out her nocturnal capers long enough for you to fall asleep? So we have something for all the members of your pack, including a shortbread and a crisp that you'll end up serving at cocktail parties, too.

Sweet dreams.

A little nothing that's still a definite something

Parmesan Shortbread

8 tablespoons (1 stick) unsalted butter, softened

1 tablespoon sugar

½ cup grated Parmigiano-Reggiano cheese (no, the salty dust that comes in a shaker will not cut the mustard)

10 grinds of black pepper or a dusting of cayenne pepper

½ teaspoon chopped lemon zest

1 teaspoon chopped fresh thyme or rosemary, optional

1 ¼ cups all-purpose flour

★

MAKES 12 PIECES

We've taken most of the sugar out of these shortbread cookies and replaced it with the fragrant nuttiness of great Parmesan cheese. Half a pear and one of these butter-rich, savory biscuits—all right, two of these, or maybe three—are a perfect pairing for a midnight treat: sweet, salt, crunch, and aaah!

These will take half an hour from start to finish, so ten minutes before the eleven o'clock news begins, mix up the dough—it takes just one bowl—and by the time the sportscaster's hyperventilating about his alma mater losing yet another game, you'll have a reason to leave for the kitchen.

For variety, you can make this shortbread with Asiago or Pecorino cheese as well.

★ Preheat the oven to 325°F. Butter and line an 8 x 8-inch pan with buttered foil or parchment paper.

★ In a mixing bowl, combine the butter, sugar, cheese, pepper, lemon zest, and optional herbs. Beat with a hand mixer until light and creamy, about 2 to 3 minutes.

★ Add the flour and mix on the lowest speed until the dough is smooth. Scrape the dough into the prepared pan and press it evenly across the bottom. Dip a fork into flour and pierce the dough randomly.

★ Bake the shortbread for 25 minutes or until firm.

★ While the shortbread is slightly warm, carefully invert the pan onto a cutting board. Remove the parchment paper and cut the shortbread into 2-inch squares.

Sugared Raisin-Bread Crisps

Here three ingredients attain a height that few bits of stale bread have ever known. It's the best way to use day-old, even week-old, bread. Pick up a loaf of pumpernickel with raisins, cranberry-walnut bread, or our preference, pecan-raisin bread. More and more bakeries and groceries are featuring these artisanal loaves.

As if the crisps weren't divine enough, we've been known to spread them with crème fraîche, cream cheese, or goat cheese—and to top that with slices of fresh figs, peaches, or pears. The only trouble is, you might want to stay up past your bedtime noshing on these.

★ ★ ★

½ loaf leftover raisin-walnut bread, thinly sliced (⅓-inch-thick slices)

8 tablespoons (1 stick) unsalted butter, melted

½ cup cinnamon sugar

★

MAKES 10 TO 12 PIECES

- ★ Preheat the oven to 350°F. Line a baking sheet with aluminum foil.
- ★ Brush both sides of the bread slices with the melted butter, then sprinkle both sides with the cinnamon sugar.
- ★ Arrange the slices on the baking sheet and bake for 10 minutes or until the sugar begins to melt. Turn the slices over and bake them for an additional 7 to 10 minutes. The bread should be caramelized and crispy.
- ★ Eat warm. Once cool, seal the crisps in an airtight container for more midnight snacks.

Chicken-Liver Biscotti

1 cup chicken livers, washed, chopped, and drained

¼ cup vegetable shortening, room temperature

1 large egg

1 tablespoon finely chopped garlic

3 cups whole wheat flour

½ teaspoon baking powder

½ teaspoon baking soda

½ cup water, as needed

½ cup cornmeal, as needed

★

MAKES 6 DOZEN BISCOTTI

Here is the ultimate bedtime snack for your dog. Sure, you can augment the recipe with hazelnuts, fennel seeds, yogurt-covered raisins, or any other nouveau ingredient you'd like, because a dog's taste is nothing if not obliging. (What are table scraps, after all?) You can also substitute chicken stock for the water and grate in smoked pigs' ears for extra flavor, but we can take no responsibility for your dog's behavior if you tempt him thusly.

These biscotti have the highest pedigree: dog trainers often use liver to focus a dog's attention, and these tidbits snap a dog to attention faster than anything store-bought. You can make thick biscuits for big rewards or thin slices to break into tidbits for training rewards. If you have a toy dog, you might want to make slender logs that will yield smaller biscotti; if you have a big beast, you might want a thicker log to toast up bigger bites.

A tin of these makes the ideal gift for other dog people in your life. So you may put this in the category of Things to Do in a Perfect World Where You Have Enough Time for Everything.

★ ★ ★

★ Preheat the oven to 350°F.

★ Use a mixer or food processor to blend together the chicken livers, shortening, egg, and garlic.

★ In a separate bowl, stir together the flour, baking powder, and baking soda with a fork.

★ Add the flour mixture to the processor gradually, pulsing to combine to create a dough. Add the water as necessary to form a sticky pink dough. (That's chicken livers for you.)

★ Dump the dough onto a counter thickly dusted with cornmeal. Divide the dough in half and use the cornmeal to help you shape two logs. Neatness does not count. Place the logs on a baking sheet as you form them. We usually make the logs 2 inches wide and 1 inch thick, but you should feel free to make them wider and a bit thicker. You can also use egg yolks and food coloring to paint pictures of mailmen or kitties on the surface—not that your dog will notice.

★ Bake for about 30 minutes or until a tester inserted into the logs comes out clean.

★ Let the logs cool for 10 minutes or until they're cool enough to handle. Leave the oven on.

★ Transfer the loaves to a cutting board and, with a sharp, serrated knife, cut them into ¼-inch slices. (This thinner biscotti will crisp up into the sort of hard biscuit dogs like crunching.) Place the slices, cut side down, on the baking sheet and bake for 15 minutes. Flip the slices and bake for another 15 minutes. You want the biscotti to be very toasted, so bake a little longer if necessary. They will harden more as they cool.

★ Store the cooled biscotti in an airtight tin. They won't last more than a couple weeks, but that's because of your dog's persistence, not the biscotti's shelf life.

Catnap Nips

1¾ cups whole wheat flour

¼ cup soy flour

⅓ cup dry milk powder

2 tablespoons wheat germ

1 teaspoon dried catnip
(available at pet shops)

1 large egg

⅓ cup whole milk

2 tablespoons vegetable oil

1 tablespoon unsulphured
molasses

★

MAKES SOMETHING LIKE
144 SNACKS (C'MON,
CAT SNACKS ARE SMALL)

We're not at all certain if there is a human equivalent of catnip—a substance that delights, intoxicates even, yet never enters the blood system, and then vanishes without any lingering effect—but we're clearly on the lookout. Meanwhile, cats have all the luck—or at least the cats who share in your bedtime rituals with their own small snack. These are the cat's meow, according to our tabby. They're nutritionally sound, take less time to make than a typical catnap, and a batch will last almost five months. Now just try to tell your cat you can't find the time to cook up two batches a year.

★ ★ ★

★ Preheat the oven to 350°F. Lightly oil a baking sheet.

★ Mix the dry ingredients together. Add the egg, whole milk, oil, and molasses. Beat until a dough forms.

★ Roll the dough on the baking sheet to a thickness of ¼ inch, which should be a 10 x 10-inch square. Score the dough into ½-inch squares or into whatever size seems right for your cat.

★ Bake for 20 minutes. Turn off the oven and allow the treats to cool in the oven for 5 minutes.

★ Break the cookies apart and return them to the baking sheet. Then it's back into the still-hot oven to dry out completely. Let the little nips stay in the oven all night if you like and pack them in an airtight container in the morning.

Why must you leave home and pay hotels hundreds of dollars simply to get sample-size shampoo bottles and a mint on your pillow? Don't you deserve a mint every night, at your own home? Or maybe you'd like to set out such a treat for a houseguest, your partner, or your kids.

Because we wanted to offer you a very quick method of making chocolates, we don't expect you to run to the store for such specialty items as pure peppermint oil, nor do we urge you to temper the chocolate, a process that keeps chocolate snappy and free from "blooming" (forming harmless but inelegant blushes of white on the surface). So if you're interested in going into business with these recipes, you'll have to stay up late tempering the chocolate, which involves firing the temperature of the cooking chocolate up and down to achieve an ideal suspension of cocoa butter, chocolate solids, and sugar. Or you can hire out the work and get yourself a good night's sleep.

★ ★ ★

★ Line an 8 x 8-inch pan with aluminum foil.

★ Crush the peppermints to a powder by placing them in a small plastic bag and hammering them with a heavy object, such as a rolling pin or the big rock at the curb that has your street number painted on it.

★ Carefully melt the semisweet chocolate and white chocolate in separate bowls over hot water. You can also use a microwave on the lowest setting for a total of 1½ minutes, then stir to complete the melting process.

★ Pour half of the semisweet chocolate into the prepared pan. Freeze for 5 minutes.

(continued on next page)

12 strong peppermint mints, such as Altoids

8 ounces best-quality semisweet chocolate, coarsely chopped, or semisweet chips

4 ounces white chocolate, coarsely chopped, or 4 ounces white chocolate chips

A drop of green food color

★

MAKES 32 PIECES

(continued)

★ Add the crushed peppermints and a drop of green food color to the melted white chocolate. Stir until the color is even. Add a drop or two more if the tint isn't green enough for you. Pour the mixture over the cold semisweet chocolate layer. Freeze for 5 minutes or until set.

★ Pour the remaining semisweet chocolate on top of the green filling and spread it evenly. (If the remaining chocolate has cooled, warm it slightly until it is smooth enough to pour.)

★ Place the finished pan in the freezer for an additional 5 minutes or until set.

★ To cut, remove the foil from the pan and slice the layered chocolate into desired shapes. The mints will keep for several days in an airtight container in the refrigerator. Separate each layer with waxed paper.

VARIATIONS

To double or triple the mintiness, add one or both of the following to the white chocolate mixture with the peppermints:

★ 2 drops of peppermint oil, if you happen to have it on hand

★ Several of those wrapped peppermint candies (about ⅓ cup total) that restaurants often offer. Check your pockets, dresser, penny drawer, etc. Those mints need another chance at a useful life.

Fireside Fodder

Remember trying to roast marshmallows on a three-foot green stick and watching them crash and burn in the blazing campfire? Remember the scouting jamboree when you wrapped a banana and chocolate in foil, wedged the packet among the ashes, sampled two bites of the molten, unbearably sweet mess, and then pitched it into the woods? Remember the family reunion at which everyone stood with watermelon slices at their faces like giant grins, spitting seeds into the dying embers of a fire just to hear that satisfying little sputter?

What is it about a campfire that inspires camaraderie? Fire seems to ignite conversation, laughter, intimacy, serenity—and if you're like our friend Douglas, a trip to the barber to even up your singed bangs. Whether it's just the two of you or a gathering, a bonfire, a campfire, or even citronella candles huddled in the center of a picnic table create the ambience for storytelling, for shucking the day's cares.

We're all for year-round bonfires. After carving pumpkins in the fall, gather friends around a fire and nestle Campfire Apples among the hot ashes. Midsummer, stall the fleeting season with a campfire circle: lie on your back and watch the fire's sparks rise and disappear as if they were joining their stellar brethren. Then bring things down to earth with some Shaggy Dogs: roasted marshmallows dipped in chocolate and rolled in coconut.

Build a winter campfire while your nephews are hot-dogging it on your frozen pond and cook up some Fire-Roasted Taters (page 55): First warm your hands with the baked pouches, then warm your insides with spoonfuls of the creamy bakers. And while you're clearing the garden come spring, run inside to brew some espresso, fill two mugs with vanilla ice cream, and come back to the fire before dumping the bitter, steaming coffee into the cold mugs. Can you think of a better image for spring's mercurial warmth and chill?

Even indoors, a fire works its magic, albeit on a more manageable scale—particularly if you have gas logs. For these contemplative or intimate moments, we offer you several mood-enhancing potables: a chai to sip while writing messages on your holiday cards, a calming tea for when you're teaching the kitty to lie in your lap without swatting the pencil, and an intense hot chocolate to savor along with the last chapter of the novel you wish would never end.

Keep those home fires burning.

Fires seem to ignite conversation

Blond Hot Chocolate

2 cups milk (see Note below)

½ teaspoon vanilla extract

4 tablespoons white
chocolate, grated

Whipped cream or
marshmallow cream

★

SERVES 2

This cup of hot white chocolate is sure to become a fireside favorite, even if you only have gas flames, plug-in glo-logs, or an urn of dried flowers behind your fire screen. It's lighter than milk or dark chocolate, and it has no caffeine to rewire you. All you need to provide is the rocking chair, the quilt, and the contented smile.

★ ★ ★

★ Pour the milk into a glass measuring cup. Heat in the microwave for 3 or 4 minutes or until it is hot. Add the vanilla.

★ Divide the grated chocolate between two mugs. Pour the hot milk mixture over the chocolate and stir.

★ Serve with a dollop of whipped cream or marshmallow cream.

NOTE: For a lighter cup, use low-fat milk. And for an even richer cup, replace ½ cup of the milk with the same amount of light cream or unsweetened coconut milk.

Yes, this is simply French for "hot chocolate," but the Gallic version is nothing like the thin, insipid chocolatey swill made by swirling dry mix in hot water. We concocted this recipe by recalling those long-ago visits to Angelina's, a famous Paris tearoom, where our miserable four quarters of college French could manage little more than ordering chocolat chaud, merci.

This is a steaming cup of molten chocolate. Brace yourself. To cut the richness, you can serve it with dollops of sweetened whipped cream.

★ ★ ★

2 cups half-and-half (okay, you can use whole milk, but the extra butterfat will elevate the experience significantly)

4 ounces dark or bittersweet chocolate, chopped (see Note below)

½ cup heavy cream, whipped with sugar, optional

Grated chocolate or cocoa powder, optional

★

SERVES 2

★ Heat 1 cup of the half-and-half in a saucepan.

★ Turn the heat to low and add the chopped chocolate. Whisk until the chocolate is entirely melted, then continue stirring another 3 minutes. The mixture should thicken a bit.

★ Add the remaining cup of half-and-half and heat until it's piping hot.

★ Pour into small mugs or cups and top with the whipped cream and chocolate shavings, if desired.

VARIATIONS

★ A tiny dash of cayenne pepper and a sprinkle of ground cinnamon added to the heating liquid shifts the taste buds into overdrive.

★ To the chocolate base you can also add brandy or a favorite liqueur, such as Kahlúa, Grand Marnier, or Frangelico.

NOTE: If you're going to down a cup of half-and-half and 2 ounces of chocolate (roughly 900 calories—that's before the additional heavy cream dollop—and a whopping lot of fat), why make this with anything but the best-quality chocolate? Vahlrona, Lindt, Côte d'Or, El Rey, and Scharffen Berger are increasingly available, and for a few more dollars you can justify that expenditure of calories and money with this extravagant sensation.

Two Vanilla Coffees

2 cups milk

2 shots hot espresso, decaffeinated if you prefer

2 teaspoons vanilla extract

Sugar

★

SERVES 2

You're comfortable at home and it's late, so why run out to a coffee shop for something you can concoct yourself? You don't need fancy bottles of Italian syrups or surly, implausibly pierced high school students to brew your day's end cup. Vanilla extract is in everyone's cupboard, and its fragrance is all about sweet dreams—oh, and ice cream.

Here are two coffees that feature vanilla in both of these forms. First, a café latte of sorts, with vanilla to lift it heavenward. And second, a mug of melding contrasts: bitter meets sweet, steaming hot meets icy cold.

Vanilla Latte

★ Heat the milk in a glass measuring cup or an earthenware mug.

★ Add the espresso along with the vanilla. Add sugar to taste.

Vanilla Iced Coffee

★ Scoop the ice cream into the chilled coffee mugs and pour the hot espresso over the top.

4 scoops best-quality vanilla-bean ice cream (who needs guar gum?)

2 shots hot strong espresso, decaffeinated if you prefer

2 coffee mugs chilled in the freezer for 10 minutes

★

SERVES 2

Brewed Cider

Perhaps brewed cider is the all-American version of chai, since both involve the mulling of spices. The scent of this warm autumnal brew evokes a feeling of peace and calm and the overwhelming realization that your lawn is dying under the leaves you've been meaning to rake.

When jugs of cider appear in the markets in the fall, pick up a gallon. Whatever you don't drink in a week or so, boil down until the liquid reduces to a thick syrup. This is delicious spread on muffins and pancakes, used as a base in marinades, or painted as a glaze on meats, fish, or various vegetables before or after grilling.

* In a 4-cup microwave-safe vessel, combine all the ingredients and blast on high for 3 minutes.
* Allow the ingredients to infuse for 5 minutes. Reheat for an additional 2 minutes and then decant the brew into mugs.

VARIATION

Instead of cider or juice, use hard cider, making this libation an entirely adult delectation. Or try a splash of brandy. Remember that Ohio's own Johnny Appleseed went about sowing apple trees for the purpose of hard-cider production, not pie making and teacher brown-nosing. Besides, in the days before refrigeration, anyone storing apples, intentionally or not, was in the applejack business.

3 cups apple cider or apple juice

2 cinnamon sticks

2 whole star anise (can be dried after steeping to use for another mulling)

Juice of 1 lemon

★

SERVES 2

Nighttime Chai

6 peppercorns

6 to 8 green cardamom pods, crushed to release their seeds

5 cloves

2 cinnamon sticks

1 teabag or tea ball full of golden Assam tea or Irish breakfast tea

1 quarter-size piece of crystallized ginger

1 to 3 tablespoons honey, to taste

2 cups milk

Anisette or orange liqueur, optional

★

SERVES 4

Chai is brewed on street corners all over India and consumed from every sort of vessel—fine porcelain cups, clay mugs, or small metal bowls. If you're intending to drive across three states before dawn, brew up a Thermos with the strongest tea; otherwise, choose decaffeinated tea. Since it takes no more time to make a generous pot of this than it does to make a single cup, brew the full pot; triple or quadruple the ingredients and add them to a teapot or a heatproof pitcher. Refrigerate any extra for the next few days' sipping.

★ ★ ★

★ Bring 2 cups of water to a boil and pour it into a teapot or heatproof pitcher with all the peppercorns, cardamom pods, cloves, cinnamon sticks, tea, ginger, and honey. Let the chai steep for 5 minutes (if you like a stronger brew, give it another couple minutes), then strain the tea into mugs.

- ★ Strain the liquid into a coffee mug, filling it halfway. Pour in an equal amount of milk. (Any unused tea will keep for several days in the refrigerator.)
- ★ Microwave the mug if you want to savor the chai hot; plunk in ice cubes to enjoy it cold.
- ★ For what coffee menus like to call "a sophisticated treat," add a splash of anisette or orange liqueur.

Campfire Apples

2 large cooking apples

¼ cup golden raisins

2 tablespoons chopped toasted nuts (almonds, walnuts, or pecans)

1 tablespoon chopped orange zest

¼ cup maple syrup or honey

2 tablespoons orange juice or apple cider

Whipped cream or ice cream, optional

★

SERVES 2

And now for all camp alumni and even for those spared the trials of outdoor cooking, an entirely gratifying treat—a fireside baked apple—that you can try the next time you're huddled around the campfire telling ghost stories. It's also easy to cook these in the backyard grill, nestling the apples among the gray briquettes. If you bake up a few extra, they'll reheat in the microwave, still holding in some of that fire-roasted taste.

★ ★ ★

★ Core the apples, and then slice the top from each one about one-quarter of the way down. Scoop out part of the apple core to make room for the filling.

★ Place each apple on a square of aluminum foil and fill each one with half the raisins, nuts, and zest.

★ Mix together the maple syrup and orange juice, then drizzle this in and around the apples. Wrap the apples securely in the foil and place on top of hot coals. Cook them until they feel tender (about 30 minutes). Let them cool, then serve with whipped cream or ice cream, if desired.

Fire-Roasted Taters

Cooking the unassuming spud over a campfire gives it a velvety texture and a subtle roasted flavor or, if you're inattentive, a bitter, charred husk with a dried, mealy center. We can't promise to hover over your coals and ensure the former, but this recipe makes success more likely, thanks to double-wrapping in foil and the butter and cream that poaches the potatoes nestled inside.

★ ★ ★

★ Quarter each potato and place 4 wedges on each of two squares of heavy-duty aluminum foil. Curl up the edges of the foil.

★ Pour 2 tablespoons of cream over each packet of potato wedges and dot them with butter. Sprinkle the potatoes with salt, pepper and chives.

★ Securely seal up the potato wedges. Go ahead and double-wrap each packet; consider it fire insurance.

★ Place the packets among the orange embers of a glowing campfire. Cook for 20 to 25 minutes or until the potato pieces are tender. Take care opening the foil packets, which will release steam.

2 medium to large russet potatoes

4 tablespoons heavy cream

2 tablespoons butter

Salt and freshly ground pepper

1 tablespoon snipped fresh chives

★

SERVES 2

Shaggy Dogs

4 to 6 large marshmallows

½ cup thin chocolate sauce

**1 cup puffed rice cereal
(such as Rice Krispies)**

★

SERVES 2

Remember how at sleep-away camp you'd slide marshmallows onto branched skewers and hold them over the campfire where you'd just endured an hour of "Kumbaya" and "The Circle Game," scrunched around the junior counselor with the guitar? Were you the patient, enviable kid who'd manage to toast an evenly browned, oozy-centered pillow, or were you the pyromaniac who'd charge from the campfire ring with a charred, flaming cinder slung from your stick?

Most often, the final product was s'mores, right? Graham crackers and chocolate bars sandwiching the hot marshmallow. But did you ever make shaggy dogs? At our camp we'd dunk the toasted marshmallow in a can of chocolate syrup and then roll the drippy mess in a box of Rice Krispies we'd have taken from the Kellogg twelve-pack designated in the overnight supply list as breakfast.

While researching this summertime treat, we found that camp graduates divide into two, well, camps. Some insist that the "dog's" shagginess came from toasted rice, while others swear that it was toasted coconut. Whichever camp you find yourself in (and we've added even more options to compound your dilemma), just remember that a little goes a long way.

★ ★ ★

★ Thread the marshmallows onto skewers or peeled green sticks and toast them over an open flame until golden brown or, if you prefer, gooey and black. Remember that marshmallows, being mostly sugar, caramelize quickly, turning from light brown to black in a matter of seconds.

★ Quickly dunk the toasted marshmallows into the chocolate sauce. Whoever loses a marshmallow in the sauce has to fold up the tent.

★ Pour the rice cereal onto a plate and roll the chocolate marshmallow in the cereal until it has coated the chocolate. No question this is a sticky, drippy process, best suited for picnic tables.

VARIATIONS

★ If you come from the coconut camp of shaggy dogs, replace the rice cereal with toasted shredded coconut.

★ Grown-ups might prefer dunking a roasted marshmallow in a sauce of melted caramels (use the microwave) or even a jar of gourmet caramel sauce. Chopped toasted pecans lend the right "shagginess" for this version.

★ Or try a butterscotch sauce with chopped peanuts.

Nightcapping

Among your repertoire of late-night dishes, there ought to be a handful of elegant little bites you can prepare ahead of time for a small gathering and then finish or simply present with a few minutes of additional heating or plating. One of our

Culinary Rules is this: Never do something in front of people that you wish you had done before they arrived. (As ever, you may apply this to any area of life.) So when friends adjourn to your house for a little nosh and a nightcap after a round of early-bird nightclubbing or the twelve-hour sale at the big department store, don't spend half of that short hour futzing around at the cutting board.

Instead, present a few of these simple dishes—a range of savory and sweet bites—which you can have ready within minutes of arriving home, before anyone dozes off or starts fretting about the babysitter. This does mean you'll have to do a bit of advance preparation, but nothing that should weigh on your shoulders or keep you from vacuuming or from throwing out the tower of mail-order catalogs on the dining room table. (You know they have nothing you need. Remember this, yet another rule: If you did not need it before you saw it, you still do not need it. Even if the item is on sale, you still do not need it. However, things that are marked half off clearance you *do* need, even if you did not realize this beforehand.)

We've included some elegant appetizers, some utterly adaptable basics, a trio of unimpeachable desserts, and a few amusements as well for those moments when fatigue sets in and yet the guests have not gone home. Some say this is the perfect time to burn the daylights out of the snacks you intended to serve and send the boors away in a cloud of smoke. But we would propose preserving your culinary reputation. Instead, trot out one of those entertaining books from the middle of the last century, when having people over was the only listing in the What-Are-We-Going-To-Do-This-Weekend section of the newspaper. Our favorite, *The Party Book* from 1939, features such classic games as Irish Whoopee, Button Button Who Hasn't Got the Button, and Drawing in the Dark, which, as you guessed, involves guests drawing something in the dark, such as a horse . . . then a rider on its back . . . then a feed sack! One round of such benign frivolity, and even the most oblivious malingerer will sense that the time to eat and run has passed.

¾ cup Clamato juice, chilled

3 ounces vodka, iced (just keep a small bottle in the freezer)

½ small cucumber, seeds removed and diced (peel the skin if it has been waxed)

Freshly ground pepper, to taste

1 teaspoon horseradish, optional

4 small oysters, freshly shucked

★

SERVES 4

You might consider this drink something like an oyster shooter, although it would be an utter shame to down it so quickly . . . and an equal shame not to be able to manage half a dozen of these drinks without paying the piper. If it's a fancy occasion, add a pearl (a large silver nonpareil) to each glass and let the guests strike it rich. As for those reluctant to belly up to the raw bar, you can replace the oyster with a cooked, chilled, and diced shrimp.

★ ★ ★

★ Mix the juice, vodka, cucumber, pepper, and horseradish, if using, in a cocktail shaker or small pitcher. Be sure everything is well chilled.

★ Place 1 oyster in each of 4 small rocks glasses and divide the cocktail among them.

★ Bring the glass to your lips, tilt back your head, and slurp.

Polenta with Scampi

Here, friends, we transform a very down-to-earth dish of cooked cornmeal into an up-scale appetizer using your favorite oxymoron, jumbo shrimp. Actually, medium-size shrimp are better for late-night dining. You simply press an uncooked shrimp into the polenta before it's firmed up: picture Mann's Chinese Theater. This is another recipe that begs for a little time earlier in the day but takes only a moment to heat when guests arrive. Broiling adds a crisp edge to the polenta—a nuttiness like corn chips—that contrasts with the sweetness of the shrimp.

- ★ Oil a 9 x 13-inch pan and line it with waxed paper or parchment.
- ★ In a medium-size bowl, mix together the lemon juice, garlic, hot sauce, and olive oil. Add the shrimp, toss, and allow them to marinate for 20 minutes.
- ★ Heat a small sauté pan on the stovetop. Add the oil and onion and cook until the onion is translucent (about 5 minutes). Season with salt and pepper.
- ★ Add the cooked onion to the warm mush, along with 2 tablespoons of the parsley and the cheese. Mix until smooth. Reserve the remaining parsley for garnishing.
- ★ Empty the mush into the prepared pan and press it into a smooth layer. Drain the shrimp and press—but do not bury—each piece in the mush, making 4 rows with 4 shrimp each. Cover the pan with plastic wrap and refrigerate for 1 hour.
- ★ Cut the mush into 16 pieces, a shrimp centered in each one. Refrigerate the pan until serving time. This is where you leave off, resuming the moment guests arrive.
- ★ Preheat the oven to 300°F.
- ★ Line a jelly-roll pan with aluminum foil and oil it lightly. Arrange the polenta pieces, without touching, on the pan and slide it onto the oven's second-highest rack.
- ★ The shrimp will cook in 8 to 10 minutes; watch for them to turn from translucent gray to opaque pink. Sprinkle the broiled squares with chopped tomato or salsa and parsley. Serve them while still warm.

Juice of ½ lemon

1 small clove garlic, minced

1 tablespoon hot sauce

2 tablespoons olive oil

16 medium shrimp, peeled, deveined if necessary

1 tablespoon extra virgin olive oil

1 small red onion, chopped

Salt and freshly ground pepper

1 recipe mush (page 181), kept hot or warmed

3 tablespoons chopped flat-leaf parsley

4 ounces soft goat cheese

1 tomato, chopped, or ½ cup salsa

★

MAKES 16 PIECES

Slow-Cooked, Soft-Scrambled Eggs

4 tablespoons (½ stick)
unsalted butter

10 large eggs or 4 whole
eggs and 10 egg whites,
slightly whisked

2 tablespoons chopped flat-
leaf parsley or chervil

2 tablespoons snipped
fresh chives

1 teaspoon minced
fresh tarragon

2 tablespoons cream

Salt and freshly
ground pepper

★

SERVES 4

If eggs are, indeed, one of nature's most perfect foods, then butter is one thing that makes perfection out of most anything Mother Nature brings to the table. With enough butter, even sautéed egg cartons are probably delicious.

It's true: Eggs are nutrient-rich, full of easy-to-digest protein, chockablock with choles-terol (darn), and when prepared in this unassuming fashion, capable of becoming a sub-lime, creamy custard. You can always mist the pan with oil and forgo the 4 tablespoons of butter—but then you'd have to rename the dish "Quick-Cooked Hard-Rubber Eggs."

Beyond the subtle fresh-herb version below, you might experiment and use these soft, buttery curds as a medium for the textures and temptations of asparagus, arti-chokes, bacon, capers, caviar, crabmeat, ham, jam, mushrooms, onion, peppers, salsa, shrimp, smoked salmon, or spinach, folding one or another cooked item into the eggs at the last moment.

★ ★ ★

* Heat a medium to large nonstick skillet over medium heat for a minute. Add the butter to the pan and allow it to melt and foam.
* Continue to heat the pan but over low heat, adding the eggs, herbs, and cream. Stir with a spatula or spoon; the cooking process will be slow and should take 15 to 20 minutes at low heat. This is not a 2-minute omelet. The eggs need time to form buttery curds.
* Add salt and pepper to taste. Serve piping hot from the pan with crispy potato skins (page 89) or a stack of buttered toast.

Tofu-ed Eggs

As an alternative to these decadent eggs, we can suggest an egg "batter" that's composed of equal parts eggs and firm tofu puréed in a blender. The mixture performs almost like beaten eggs, and it bumps up the protein, lowers the fat, halves the cholesterol, and creates a creamy, somewhat paler mixture that performs well in omelets and most other egg dishes. Just keep two things in mind: First, the tofu-egg blend will tend to stick to the skillet more than eggs alone, so watch the skillet carefully and use whatever shortening you need to keep the mixture from adhering. Second, the tofu may exude a bit of water during the cooking, necessitating a slotted spoon for serving the scrambled eggs or a bit of blotting during the last stage of omelet making.

Far-Flung Turkey Hash

4 tablespoons (½ stick) unsalted butter

¼ cup all-purpose flour

2 cups chicken broth

Several dashes of favorite hot sauce

3 tablespoons olive oil

1 cup chopped red onion

1 red or green bell pepper, chopped

2 cups roasted turkey meat, cut into 1-inch pieces, or 1 pound ground turkey, cooked and drained

3 sweet potatoes, baked or boiled, peeled, and cubed

One 4-ounce can diced green chilies

This is not the sort of hash you sling. This is a superb but substantial enhancing of turkey and sweet potatoes to serve up with pride. You utilize some precooked bits, supplement them with well-chosen herbs and vegetables, and bring the whole dish together with a touch of cream and broth. A large dollop of this hash makes for a satisfying Sunday supper or a hearty winter lunch. But since you're serving it so close to midnight, a cupful will suffice. Remember that turkey brings to the table its tryptophan, an essential amino acid that potently contributes to post-Thanksgiving-dinner drowsiness.

★ ★ ★

★ Preheat the oven to 350°F and butter a 4-quart baking dish.

★ In a saucepan, melt the butter over medium heat. Whisk in the flour and stir for 3 minutes.

★ Blend in the broth and then increase the heat and boil until the sauce thickens. Add the hot sauce and set aside.

★ In a large skillet or Dutch oven, heat the oil over medium-high heat. Add the chopped onion and pepper and sauté until the onion is translucent (about 5 minutes).

- ★ Add the turkey, potatoes, chilies, garlic, paprika, ground pepper, thyme, and salt. Stir over medium heat until all the ingredients are combined.
- ★ Taste for seasoning. Stir in the reserved sauce, then spoon the turkey mixture into the prepared baking dish. Pour the half-and-half over the mixture and bake for 35 minutes.
- ★ Remove from the oven, stir in the chopped scallions and parsley, and sling.

VARIATIONS

- ★ Use smoked duck instead of or along with the turkey. Or try smoked turkey.
- ★ Create an alternate kind of hash using corned beef, chopped and quickly heated in the mix. Leave out the salt, since the meat is already salty from pickling.
- ★ Add a can of hominy or white, cannellini, or black beans. Be sure to drain and rinse the beans well.

2 tablespoons chopped garlic

1 teaspoon paprika

**1 teaspoon freshly
ground pepper**

**½ teaspoon dried thyme or
2 teaspoons fresh
thyme leaves**

1 teaspoon salt

½ cup half-and-half

4 scallions, chopped

**1 bunch flat-leaf parsley,
coarsely chopped**

★

SERVES 4

Bedtime Blini

1 egg, at room temperature

1½ cups whole milk, at room temperature

3 tablespoons unsalted butter, melted

½ teaspoon salt

½ cup all-purpose flour

½ cup buckwheat flour

Filling (see the Filling Options that follow)

★

MAKES 16 CREPES

Blini are classic, humble vehicles for dollops of crème fraîche paved with delicate slices of smoked salmon or thimblefuls of caviar. We have further glorified these ovals by creating a thinner, crêpe-like version instead of the more familiar pancake-thick blini.

The best thing about these blini, other than the refined taste, is that they can be made ahead of time and simply warmed on low in the oven in the time it takes to open the champagne and find the darned cocktail napkins. Simply prepare the blini in advance and stack the cooled cakes with pieces of waxed paper or parchment between them. Place the stack in a heavy-gauge plastic bag, squeeze out as much air as possible, and freeze.

Alternately, you can make the batter ahead, store it in the fridge, and then fry up the blini as soon as you come home from whatever nighttime escapade has taken you away.

★ Beat the egg lightly in a mixing bowl. Whisk in the milk, butter, and salt.

★ Combine the flours in a sieve and sift them into the batter, whisking until smooth. Let the batter rest for 1 hour at room temperature or for several hours in the refrigerator.

★ Mist a 6-inch nonstick skillet or crêpe pan with cooking spray and set it over medium-high heat. Pour 2 tablespoons of batter into the pan, tipping it to cover the surface evenly. Cook until the blini's edges begin to brown and the center of the pancake sets.

★ Turn the pancake and continue to cook until the underside is lightly browned. Turn the blini onto an ovenproof plate and cover it with a cotton towel. Place the plate in a warm oven set on the lowest setting.

★ Repeat the process with the remaining batter; the pan may need to be sprayed after each pancake.

★ To serve, place a bit of filling down the center of each warm blini and lift each side across the filling as if you were folding a letter.

FILLING OPTIONS

These blini can be rolled around all sorts of savory fillings:

★ Caviar or smoked salmon and crème fraîche (see page 163)

★ Cooked vegetables enhanced with a spoonful of goat cheese

★ And if you're in the mood for something sweet, use this same batter to create a thin pancake that you can stud with fresh blueberries or chopped chocolate bits.

Macaroon Sandwich Cookies

3 egg whites

¾ cup sugar

3 cups unsweetened coconut flakes (if you must use the sweetened kind, add ¼ cup flour)

If the only macaroons you've ever tasted are those sodden kosher-for-Passover nuggets that arrive in a tin, you won't be able to imagine the toasted nuttiness of these gems. Macaroons may well be the fastest cookies to prepare, with the least amount of cleanup: a single bowl and spoon. Yes, there are egg whites to separate, but no beating them into submission. And while you can subsist on the macaroon alone, the chocolate filling gives this everyday fare some real fanfare.

★ ★ ★

CHOCOLATE FILLING

¼ cup heavy cream

4 ounces semisweet chocolate, finely chopped or grated

2 tablespoons unsalted butter, at room temperature

★

★ Preheat the oven to 350°F. Line baking sheets with parchment paper.

★ In a mixing bowl, combine all the egg whites, sugar, and coconut.

★ Drop the cookie mixture by tablespoonfuls onto the baking sheets. Flatten each round slightly.

★ Bake for 10 minutes and then cool the macaroons.

★ To make the chocolate filling, in a small saucepan, bring the cream to a boil. Remove the pan from the heat.

★ Add the grated chocolate bits and butter. Stir until smooth, then refrigerate until thick enough to spread between the macaroons.

★ Once the chocolate filling has thickened, spread it between pairs of macaroons.

MAKES 18 MACAROONS

VARIATIONS

⋆ A more festive presentation, mezzaluna macaroons, takes no more effort. Instead of sandwiching the chocolate inside the macaroons, dip half of each cooled macaroon into the chocolate before it has chilled and thickened. Set these half moons on waxed paper to harden.

⋆ If you have prepared chocolate frosting, you can substitute that if no one's looking. Or you can dip or drizzle the macaroons with melted dark, white, or milk chocolate.

⋆ Not in the mood for chocolate? These macaroons are just as delicious sandwiched with lemon curd or, while still warm and soft, pressed into a crumble of pecans or hazelnuts.

Chocolate Sour Cherry Cake

10 ounces dark or bittersweet
chocolate, chopped

1 cup (2 sticks)
unsalted butter

5 large eggs

1 teaspoon vanilla extract

1 ¼ cups granulated sugar

5 tablespoons
all-purpose flour

1½ teaspoons baking powder

6 ounces dried sour cherries,
plumped (see sidebar)

Confectioners' sugar
for dusting

★

MAKES 1 SWELL CAKE

This cake does take a little time to prepare—but, look, at least you don't have to stiffen egg whites, cream butter and sugar, or even haul out the electric mixer. So for a little effort, you'll have a cake with the power to woo friends and influence people. This is a dessert you can pull from the oven right as you leave for the movies or your next-door neighbor's daughter's band recital at the fairgrounds that, inexplicably, you promised two months ago you wouldn't dream of missing. The cooled cake is ready to slice the moment you walk in the door. Whipped cream, ice cream, or chocolate sauce will hardly be necessary, although why not offer?

★ ★ ★

★ Preheat the oven to 325ºF. Coat a 10-inch springform pan with cooking spray and line the bottom of the pan with parchment paper. Spray the parchment, too.

★ In a small heatproof bowl, melt the chocolate and butter together over warm water or in the microwave on the lowest power. Cool slightly.

★ Blend the eggs, vanilla, and sugar in a large mixing bowl, whisking the mixture until it's thick and pale yellow.

- Sift in the flour and baking powder and stir to combine. Add the cooled chocolate-butter mixture and the cherries and fold together to form a batter.
- Pour the batter into the prepared pan and bake for 20 minutes. Cover the pan with foil and bake for an additional 25 minutes.
- Remove the foil and cool on a rack for 10 minutes. Once cooled, release the cake from the pan, and, when completely cooled, dust with confectioners' sugar.

Plumping Up Dried Fruit

Sometimes dried fruits are so shriveled and leathery they need rejuvenation. (You know the feeling.) Simply pour boiling water over the dried fruit—just enough to cover—and let the fruit stew for 10 to 15 minutes. Drain off the liquid and then add the fattened fruit to the recipe. To increase the fruit's flavor, add a splash of brandy or rum when you pour on the boiling water.

The Pavlova Variations

2 cups fresh fruit, sliced or
diced as required

Brandy or Grand Marnier

4 large egg whites (½ cup)

Pinch of salt

1 cup superfine
sugar

1 teaspoon vanilla extract

1 tablespoon cornstarch

2 teaspoons white vinegar

1 cup heavy cream, whipped
with 2 tablespoons sugar

★

SERVES 6

The legacy of the great Russian danseuse Anna Pavlova, best remembered for her performance in the ballet Swan Lake, *lives on in this Austrian dessert of stiffened egg whites. She deserves more. Still, this acclaimed dish has been served at grand occasions for decades and certainly ought to be among your standby dishes. It can be done up as fancy as a ballerina's costume or as casual as a workout leotard. The baked meringues are great crunchy accompaniments for poached fruit. They can provide a base for drizzled fruit sauces or warmed chocolate. Add ½ cup chopped pecans or ¼ cup chocolate chips before preparing the meringues for the baking sheet, and you'll have a very light cookie.*

Traditionally, these shells are complemented by bananas, papayas, pineapples, and mango, but we urge you to think of them as a nest for whatever you'd like to lay in them. Baked meringues will stay fresh in an airtight tin for weeks; you have them waiting backstage, as it were, ready in an instant to appear in a brief dessert performance.

★ ★ ★

★ Preheat the oven to 225°F. Line a baking sheet with parchment paper or aluminum foil.

★ Put the fruit in a bowl, splash it with the brandy, and place the bowl in the refrigerator while the fruit macerates.

★ In the bowl of an electric mixer, whip the egg whites on medium speed until they are frothy. Add the pinch of salt and continue beating until soft peaks are formed.

★ Add the sugar, 1 tablespoon at a time, and beat the whites on high speed until stiff peaks have formed.

★ Whisk in the vanilla, cornstarch, and vinegar.

★ Form the meringue into shells using one of the methods described on page 73. Bake for about 2 hours, or until the meringues are crispy but not brown. It's a slow heating process to dry out the egg whites.

★ Fill the cooled meringues with the macerated fruit and whipped cream and serve.

NOTES: To form the meringue into shapes, we offer you three choices:

★ *Almost no effort:* Place large spoonfuls of the meringue on the baking sheet. Using the back of a spoon, smooth a large depression in each foamy meringue.

★ *A little more effort:* Draw 6-inch circles on a piece of parchment paper and then flip the paper over. Fill a pastry bag fitted with a plain or fluted #6 tip (or use a large zippered plastic bag and snip off ¼ inch of one corner) and pipe the mixture inside the drawn circles. Add another ring of meringue around the circle's perimeter to form a cup. The piping takes a little extra time, but it ensures the meringues will cook evenly.

★ *Impress your friends with your own* Swan Lake *performance:* This is the venerable haute cuisine method. Create a wintery pond with individual swans lighting upon the frosty pool (use the mirror from your vanity). Use various pastry tips in order to pipe the meringue into teardrops (bodies), French curves (neck and head), and spheres (optional Frosty the Snowman—not part of the original ballet). Use a serrated knife to carve the baked shells into wings; try for delicate feathering. Use sugar and confectioners' sugar to make everything look glittery and frosty, including the kitchen. You can use brown sugar to suggest slush. We apologize for providing less than complete instructions here, but at one point we had a big argument over whether or not it was fair to use a hot-glue gun and just gave up, figuring that if you are, indeed, the overly creative type, you'll just put on the Tchaikovsky ballet and wing it.

The Bewitching Hour

Midnight is the witching hour, when P.M. becomes A.M., the clock hands come together in a hallelujah overhead, and the computer suddenly designates the project you're working on as "yesterday." It's the hour when the fitness models invade the channels with their slimmerizing ab machines and the VCR finally tells its one truth. Big changes are taking place, not that you're going to transform into the Wolf Man and roam the neighborhood, but something is afoot.

Perhaps you're with a new love. At midnight you want more than water at your oasis. You want impressive but instantaneous temptations to share, some silly halftime snack so you can get back to your pajama games. Try the melon spears soaked in anisette with mint for a tantalizing diversion. Perhaps you're alone. It's midnight and the election results are still trickling in—you aren't throwing in the towel yet. Or you're icing 100 gingerbread men for your daughter's school's fundraiser tomorrow, and she insists they all need really cute faces. You're hungry for anything besides gingerbread. Try a halved plum baked with goat cheese and sprinkled with pine nuts and pepper. Two bounteous flavor bursts, and no burden at all. Perhaps you and your spouse are staying up to watch the lunar eclipse or the beauty pageant you can't believe you got sucked into watching, since your state's contestant was eliminated in the evening-wear round. Or it's the driveway's automatic floodlights you're watching that will signal your daughter's date has kept his promise. You need more than subsistence fare: you want food for team spirit, moral support, inner fortitude. Try a pair of thin omelets with torn sheets of nori seaweed, which you roll like a burrito and munch with the same convenient ease.

Or maybe you'll decide to pan-fry risotto cakes, fashion ladyfingers into a fast-track tiramisu, or erect your own trifle tower. You'll master all these fancies with your first attempt. There's nothing to bewitch, bother, or bewilder you this close to bedtime.

nothing to bewitch, bother, or bewilder

6 sun-dried tomatoes, chopped, or 2 tablespoons chopped fresh basil

1 cup cooked risotto, cooled

Freshly ground pepper

¼ cup cornmeal for dredging cakes, optional

Vegetable oil for pan-frying

Freshly grated Parmigiano-Reggiano cheese for dusting, optional

★

MAKES 6 CAKES

This is the consummate way to recast leftover risotto—in fact, the recipe for creating risotto in the microwave (see recipe that follows) is so easy, you'll be tempted to cook a whole batch of "leftovers" just so you can fry up these crisp patties.

The key to this dish—what we hesitate to call the "crispification"—is creating the crunchy, intense flavor of browned and baked grains on the outside while preserving the creamy grains inside. You want to fry the cakes to harden both sides of the cheesy rice until they resemble the crunchy layer that forms on the bottom of a superlatively pre-pared paella that's always offered to the guest of honor.

But why wait for your turn to be guest of honor? With this recipe everyone can have a cake and eat it, too.

★ ★ ★

★ Gently mix the tomatoes or the basil into the cooled risotto.

★ Form the risotto into six balls the size of walnuts, then press to flatten each disk until it is about ⅓ inch thick. Take a moment to smooth the edges of the cakes so that they will retain their shape when you flip them.

★ Quickly blot the cakes in a plate of cornmeal. Roll the edges in cornmeal, too. This adds to the nuttiness of the crust, but it's not essential.

★ Heat a griddle pan or a nonstick skillet over high temperature. Add a small amount of oil and wait for it to heat up. Lower heat to medium-high. Pan-fry the cakes on each side, allowing them to become golden brown and crisp (about 2 minutes). To keep the exterior crisp, don't stack the cakes.

★ Serve the cakes immediately, dusting with more cheese if you're so inclined. If after eating the three you thought would surely suffice, you want the three others sitting on the counter, crisp them again with a quick second searing in the skillet.

Microwave Risotto

Infinitely suited for last-minute late-night pursuits, a risotto can be prepared, cooked, and served in the same microwave-safe bowl. This is the traditional Italian rice dish but without the prolonged stirring at the stove (or the lovely conversations and glass of wine that usually go along with the languid stirring).

* In a microwave-safe bowl, combine the chopped onion and shortening. Microwave on high for 4 minutes, stirring once after 2 minutes.
* Add the rice and stir to coat the grains with the oil. Microwave on high for 4 more minutes.
* Add the chicken broth and return the bowl to the microwave. Let the rice cook at high power for 18 minutes, stirring once halfway through. Stir again before the last 2 minutes, checking to see that the liquid is almost absorbed.
* Remove the bowl from the microwave and let the rice absorb the final bit of liquid. Stir 2 or 3 times.
* Add the cheese. Check the seasoning and then add both salt and pepper.
* Before serving, you can add minced herbs, swirl in a pat of butter, or for a creamier, more porridge-like risotto, stir in a little milk or cream.

VARIATIONS

Since the above recipe suggests only the foundation of this broadly interpretable dish, consider these supplements:

* Add a pinch of saffron threads or ground dried mushrooms to the broth.
* Stir cooked vegetables, such as asparagus bits or grilled corn, into the finished rice.
* Exchange ½ cup of the chicken stock for white wine or cream.
* Sprinkle on a small handful of chopped fresh herbs at the end of cooking (flat-leaf parsley, thyme, rosemary, and/or basil).

1 small onion or 2 shallots, chopped

3 tablespoons extra virgin olive oil or butter, or a mixture of both

1 cup Arborio rice

3 cups chicken stock

½ cup grated Parmigiano-Reggiano cheese

Salt and freshly ground pepper

Minced fresh herbs, butter, milk, or cream, optional

Egg Roll-Ups

2 teaspoons vegetable oil (you can also use hot chili oil or sesame oil to replace part of the blander vegetable oil)

2 shallots or scallions (white part only), finely chopped

1 tablespoon chopped fresh flat-leaf parsley, cilantro, chives, or chervil

4 large eggs, lightly beaten

Salt and freshly ground pepper

★

MAKES 2 ROLL-UPS

FILLING OPTIONS

Sour cream, sautéed mushrooms, and shallots

Sliced fontina cheese, prosciutto, and chopped cooked spinach

Chopped scallions, bean sprouts, sesame seeds, and soy sauce

Slivers of Parmigiano-Reggiano cheese

A very thin omelet rolled around a fresh and uncomplicated filling provides a minor miracle for midnight consumption. We've suggested an "eggaletarian" preparation for everyday snacking, as well as an "eggstravagant" version for company. Let these egg you on to more variations and worse puns.

Everyday Egg Roll-ups

★ In a large nonstick skillet, heat the oil over medium heat. Add the chopped shallots or scallions and cook until they are soft. Remove half of the cooked shallots from the pan and set aside for making the second roll.

★ Mix the herbs into the eggs and pour half of the mixture into the pan. Tilt the pan to coat the bottom evenly. Cook the eggs over medium heat until they are set—less than a minute.

★ Sprinkle with salt and pepper and slide the egg disk onto a plate. Place a small amount of a filling on one side of the disk, then roll it into a tube for easy munching.

★ Return the reserved cooked shallots to the skillet and repeat the procedure to make another roll-up.

Maki-Style Omelets With Nori or Herbs

This same egg dish can be dressed up for guests, producing something of a hybrid between Japanese tamago sushi (the sweet egg bar) and maki, or rolled, sushi. Our version includes seafood options, a lighter evening fare, and is equally good alone or with a variety of enhancements.

★ ★ ★

★ In a large nonstick skillet, heat the oil over medium heat. Add the shallots or scallions and cook until they are soft. Remove half of the cooked shallots from the pan and set aside for making the second roll.

★ Mix the fish sauce and nori or herbs into the eggs and pour half the mixture into the pan. Tilt the pan to coat the bottom evenly. Cook the eggs over medium heat until they are just set—less than 1 minute. Slide the egg disk onto a small sheet of waxed or parchment paper.

★ Return the reserved cooked shallots to the skillet and repeat the procedure to make another egg disk.

★ Carefully spread your choice of filling over each disk, then roll it up.

★ Using the waxed paper, seal each roll tightly, as though the paper were a sausage casing. Microwave the rolls for 30 seconds.

★ Cutting on a bias, slice through the paper and separate each roll into four pieces.

★ Remove the paper and set two pieces on each of four plates. For enhancement's sake, nap with melted butter and, if you like, surround the pieces with roasted red pepper sauce, tomato sauce, or even a hedge of salad greens tossed with vinaigrette.

½ teaspoon fish sauce (a salty condiment found at Asian markets and larger groceries)

1 sheet toasted nori (Japanese seaweed used in making sushi), cut into strips, or whole leaves of fresh herbs (basil, tarragon, flat-leaf parsley, chervil, or dill)

★

MAKES 8 PIECES

FILLINGS

Ricotta cheese, smoked salmon, dill, capers, and red onion

Smoked fish, cream cheese, and fresh herbs

Spinach, feta cheese, nutmeg, and pine nuts

Macerated Melons with Anisette and Mint

½ cantaloupe or honeydew
or both, peeled, seeded, and
cut into long spears

½ cup anisette liqueur,
such as Pernod

¼ cup sugar

Freshly ground pepper

Zest of 1 lemon,
finely chopped

2 tablespoons coarsely
chopped fresh mint

★

SERVES 4

Each summer a phone rings out late one evening: it's our friends Rodger and Jennie. The night-blooming cereus summering on their front porch is about to bloom. Also known as queen of the night, the massive plant offers up only a few blooms, only once a year, and each flower lasts less than a whole night. But it's worth climbing out of bed and driving over to witness: a blossom as intricate as cutwork linen, as opulent as an alabaster carving, and as outrageously fragrant as anything else the giddy plant kingdom has evolved.

Lucky friends are treated not only to the extravagant efflorescence but also to a few of Jennie's midnight snacks, including this marinated melon, whose licorice-scented perfume is as profound as that of the cereus.

Serve this to your guests even if you don't have such a botanical wonder; put on The Magic Flute *and listen to the musical wonder of Mozart's* Queen of the Night.

★ ★ ★

★ Place the ½ cantaloupe or honeydew, or ¼ of both, sugar, and liqueur in a locking plastic bag. Sprinkle with pepper and the lemon zest. Toss in the mint. Close the bag with as little air as possible to keep the liquid in contact with the melon.

★ Allow the melon to macerate in the refrigerator for as long as you can resist; all day is fine. Gently rotate the spears a couple of times, shifting them inside the plastic bag.

★ Serve the melon spears cold. Reserve the marinade for additional melon pieces or pour it into a highball glass with a few cubes of ice and sip slowly.

Just a Trifle

Trifles can be trifled with. The concept is elementary: Find a tall sundae or pilsner glass to provide the towering effect that's part of this treat's experience, and scrounge around your kitchen for the ideal layers you'll need—something sweet and dry, something fresh and juicy, and then something creamy to make it all dreamy.

We begin with the classic British version, which we offer as our basic trifle to remind you of the proportions you'll want. Once you're tempted by the variations, you can pick and choose from among the ingredients we've listed, using your own sense of taste and proportion.

1 cup spoon-size pieces pound cake

1 cup fresh berries

¼ cup berry sauce (or purée berries with some confectioners' sugar to taste)

¼ cup whipped cream

★

SERVES 1

★ ★ ★

★ In a tall glass, alternate cake, berries, and sauce—try for two layers of each, anyway—topping off the tower with whipped cream.

VARIATIONS

Tropical Tower: Use gingerbread or pound cake and alternate it with layers of toasted coconut shreds, butterscotch sauce, coconut ice cream or pineapple sherbet, dark rum or orange juice, and a tropical fruit, such as papaya, banana, or mango.

Grandma's Old-Fashioned Trifle: Layer a parfait glass with crumbled molasses cookies or gingerbread cookies, apples or pears sautéed in a bit of butter, cognac, caramel sauce, and vanilla ice cream.

Oats and Berries: Break up crunchy oatmeal cookies and build your dessert with sliced nectarines and blueberries, whipped cream, maple syrup, and brandy.

Animal Crackers in My Goop: For a children's hour treat, use whole animal crackers or broken Danish butter cookies, pecans or walnuts, chocolate syrup, vanilla yogurt, and candy pieces, such as crushed malted-milk balls, M&Ms, Zagnuts, Butterfingers, or Twix.

¼ cup freshly brewed dark
coffee (a spoonful of
instant espresso coffee
will also work)

1½ ounces dark rum or coffee
liqueur, such as Kahlúa

7 ladyfingers (we prefer
the crisp, Italian-style)

1 spoonful of mascarpone
cheese (see Note below)

Semisweet chocolate peels
(use a vegetable peeler to
scrape a block of chocolate)

★

**MAKES 1 HUNGRY-SIZE
SERVING OR 2 SMALLER
SERVINGS**

In Italian, tiramisu translates as "pick-me-up," and this Tuscan trifle is never served for dessert—except in tourist restaurants. Instead, tiramisu is what Italians munch on between an insubstantial breakfast of café latte and a big pasta lunch around one. It's their midmorning momentum booster: a sugar and caffeine rush that keeps those ubiquitous cell phones and Vespas running.

In our stateside, late-side version, you can assemble a peremptorily delicious variation in the time it takes to rewind the video. And considering the late hour, use decaffeinated espresso unless you're planning to be up at 4:30 A.M. for stuffed manicotti.

★ ★ ★

★ Combine the coffee and rum.

★ Place three ladyfingers across a plate and drizzle with a third of the liquid. Dab with a third of the cheese.

★ Place two more ladyfingers crisscrossing the bottom layer and add half of the remaining liquid and half of the remaining cheese.

★ Place the last two ladyfingers crisscrossing the middle layer and pour on the last of the liquid as well as the final dollop of cheese.

★ Top with peels of chocolate—and laughter.

NOTE: For a last-minute mascarpone, you can stir together a little half-and-half or whipping cream with some softened cream cheese.

Visions of chèvre Plums

Whether you bake up greengages, Stanleys, damsons, Santa Rosas, or any other plums, these jewels can be the sunny-side-up center of a midnight meal for two. Scrumptious with a glass of grappa and a biscotti, these warm, tart bites can also enliven a bed of mixed greens tossed lightly with a vinaigrette dressing. In any case, these dolloped drupes are anything but plum tuckered out.

★ ★ ★

2 whole plums

2 tablespoons goat cheese

1 tablespoon pine nuts

1 tablespoon sweet vermouth or grappa

Freshly ground pepper

★

MAKES 4 PIECES

- ★ Preheat the oven to 350ºF. Lightly oil a small ceramic or ovenproof glass dish.
- ★ Cut the plums in half and remove the pits. Smash the goat cheese into the cut surface of the halves and top with pine nuts. Place the plum pieces in the dish and sprinkle them with the vermouth and the pepper.
- ★ Bake for 15 to 20 minutes, until the cheese melts and the fruit begins to soften. Serve warm. Savor. Swoon.

VARIATION

When fresh figs suddenly appear in the market, give them a tour of duty in this same dish, replacing the goat cheese with a mild blue cheese.

12:15 AM

Crunches
Before Bed

You've just arrived home from the city's fireworks display, enduring a traffic jam that lasted four times as long as the pyrotechnic display. You're up waiting for your daughter to come home from band practice in the neighbor's garage. You're memorizing lines for an audition tomorrow. You didn't end up using the opera tickets your parents gave you. You thought about it. You also thought about sorting your expense receipts into little piles (since, once again, you've broken your vow to keep up with them weekly). And now you have the munchies.

What is better for the midnight munchies than something crunchy? But alas, crunch so often means deep-fried or burned, neither of which we thought, in our heart of hearts, you'd really want at this hour. Indeed, when we began this book, we insisted on certain inviolable conditions: the terms by which all midnight cookery must abide. No barbecuing. No smoking. (No, Sharon, not even on the porch with the little hibachi that uses newspaper and hardly makes any smoke at all.) No pastry bags with multiple tips. Nothing that requires rising, larding, de-boning, blanching in three changes of water, de-scaling, de-bearding, de-greasing, wind-drying, or—hardest of all to concede—deep-frying.

We both agreed, however, that we had to find a way to include those satisfyingly brittle little nibbly bits the teeth so love chomping. We wanted something with snap, something gratifying . . . okay, we wanted corn chips and potato chips. So we set out for innovations beyond our friend Debbie's sautéed tater stix, which we understand carried her through her college years: packets of those pick-up-sticks-shaped potatoes, dumped into a skillet, sautéed in melted butter, and finally salted—essentially doubling the fat and salt while holding the potato content to a minimum.

Here, then, are several crisp alternatives to sacks of salty deep-fried chips, including two potato pleasers, sweetened tortillas, salami-turned-jerky, and a "chip" forged from little more than cheese. You'll never look at puffed cheese doodles the same way.

those satisfy-ing brittle little nibbly bits

Parmesan Wafers

1 tablespoon flour

Freshly ground pepper

1 small sprig fresh rosemary, chopped

2 ounces Parmigiano-Reggiano cheese, finely grated (but not dust)

★

MAKES 20 WAFERS

You know how, when you're making grilled cheese sandwiches or lasagna or pizza, there are always a few bits of cheese that leak out the edges and harden? Are those the most delicious crispins or what? Well, this recipe is a way to bring those wayward cheese chips center stage. In Italy they are known as frico. *They are, as cookbook writers like to say, addictive.*

★ ★ ★

★ Preheat the oven to 400ºF. Line a baking sheet with parchment paper or use a non-stick liner.

★ With a fork, toss the flour, pepper, and rosemary together and then scramble in the cheese.

★ For each wafer, sprinkle 1 tablespoon of cheese mixture onto the pan, forming a 3-inch round.

★ Bake the rounds until they're light golden brown, 4 to 5 minutes. Let them cool slightly, then remove them from the pan with a spatula and set on paper towels to blot a bit of the oil.

A FANCIFUL VARIATION

To form cheese *tuiles* (a shape inspired by French roof tiles), remove the warm wafers from the pan and drape each over a rolling pin to curl.

If you feel like forming cheese Tours Eiffel, you're simply overtired. A good night's rest will put things into perspective.

VARIATIONS

* Asiago cheese works as nicely as the Parmigiano-Reggiano.
* Add finely grated lemon zest.
* Replace the rosemary with a ½ teaspoon of chopped fresh basil, thyme, or chives.
* Try a version with a dash of paprika and 1 tablespoon of flax seeds.

Crisped Salami Chips

Thin slices of cured meat, such as salami, sopressata, pepperoni, or ham

Since all that's required here is a single ingredient, bake just as much as you think you'll want at one sitting. You can use salami, sopressata, prosciutto—in other words, your basic Italian fatty meat. (Tempted though you may be, you cannot substitute sliced turkey or chicken; the resulting meat will be as edible as peeled paint.) The good news for late-night eating is that baking removes a good deal of the meat's fat.

These crisps are also terrific crumbled into salads—a cross between ramen noodles and bacon bits—or put out at a party among those other unusual chips popping up at gourmet markets, such as sesame blue tortillas, taro or beet chips, and various oven-baked crisps.

★ ★ ★

★ Preheat the oven to 350°F.

★ Line a baking sheet with parchment paper or aluminum foil and arrange the meat slices in a single layer. Cover with a second sheet of parchment. If you are cooking many slices, you can add another layer of meat on top of this and cover with a third sheet of parchment.

★ Bake for 15 to 20 minutes, until the slices are crispy and most of the fat has been rendered. Feel free to blot a bit with a paper towel.

★ Remove the parchment and peel the crispy chips free. Serve warm.

Crispy Potato Spoons

Attention midnight snackers: If it's no surprise that you're famished at this hour, think ahead. Since baked potatoes are a fine candidate for snacking, bake a few extra at dinnertime just for these late-night urgencies.

With this recipe you can transmute an unassuming spud into a crispy, edible utensil—a scoop or a spoon—that's ready for dips, salsas, raitas, hummus, or most any savory treat. And when the occasion calls for entertaining, these bites are especially grand filled with caviar and crème fraîche.

★ ✶ ★

★ Preheat the oven to 400ºF.

★ Cut each potato in half. Scoop out the flesh, leaving a thin layer on the skin. (Save the flesh for dinner tomorrow.) Take some care not to tear through the potato's shell. Cut each potato shell in half lengthwise; then halve each half. Now you have eight long spears per potato.

★ Spray a baking sheet with cooking spray. Arrange the potato pieces in a single layer and spritz them with cooking spray. Sprinkle with salt and pepper.

★ Bake the potato shells for 10 minutes. Shake the pan and then return it to the oven for an additional 5 to 6 minutes, until the shells are golden and crispy.

★ Dust the warm shells with grated cheese, if you like. While still warm, take them for a dip.

2 large russet potatoes, baked

Salt and freshly ground pepper

Parmesan cheese, grated, optional

★

MAKES 16 PIECES

Sweet Potato Oven Fries

1 large sweet potato, peeled and cut into ½-inch-thick **batons** (a.k.a. French fries)

1 egg white, beaten until frothy

1 tablespoon vegetable oil

Salt

Malt vinegar or cinnamon sugar, optional

✳

SERVES 1

We thought of naming these "consolation fries," since they're what we eat when deep-fried or even pan-fried potatoes might be imprudent. But these are too good to confine to late-night hours. Equally delicious with a malt-vinegar splash or a sprinkling of cinnamon sugar, the sweet potato's caramel-like flavor is intensified by a brief but intense blast of heat.

If, by chance, you have a convection oven, you can bake up extra-crispy fries. If you have butter, marshmallow bits, and pineapple chunks, you can make Aunt Lulu's candied sweet potatoes instead, but then you might as well get out the deep-fryer.

★ ★ ★

* Preheat oven to 500ºF. Coat a small baking pan with cooking spray.
* Toss the sweet potato sticks with the egg white, dump them into a strainer, and tap off the extra liquid.
* Place the potatoes in the coated pan. Give each one some personal space and sprinkle with salt.
* Bake the potato sticks for 15 to 17 minutes, turning them at least once during the process. You want the sticks to be golden brown and tender.
* Sprinkle with malt vinegar or cinnamon sugar, if you like.

You may start by thinking corn chips, but without the fat, just to trigger your senses. They do share a common origin with these crackers. But these ephemeral full-moons are in a different universe than those salty, greasy curls. Here, the creamy grits that make for hearty breakfast fare undergo a virtual apotheosis into brittle, buttery circles, and all it takes is half an hour of baking. Prepare to be converted.

⋆ ★ ⋆

- ⋆ Preheat the oven to 400°F. Line two baking sheets with aluminum foil and butter the foil. (You can also use silicone liners, which don't require buttering.)
- ⋆ Combine the water and salt in a medium saucepan and bring to a rollicking boil. Add the cornmeal, using a whisk to prevent lumps from forming.
- ⋆ Reduce the heat to low and stir the mush for 10 minutes with a wooden spoon. Let the mixture simmer for an additional 10 minutes, stirring occasionally.
- ⋆ Add the paprika and butter.
- ⋆ Spoon generous tablespoons of the soft, warm mush onto the prepared baking sheets. With the back of a spoon, smear each dollop of batter into a very thin 3-inch round.
- ⋆ Bake for 25 minutes, or until the crackers are golden brown and crispy.
- ⋆ Cool the crackers on racks. Whatever is left after you've finished remarking how incredible they taste—and they're nothing more than cornmeal and butter—can be stored in an airtight container.

3 cups water

1 teaspoon salt

1½ cups yellow cornmeal

½ teaspoon paprika

4 tablespoons (½ stick) butter

★

MAKES 20 TO 25 CRACKERS

Sugar Crisps with Fruit Salsa

Two 8-inch flour tortillas

1 egg white

2 tablespoons sugar

½ teaspoon ground cinnamon, optional

¼ cup walnuts, finely chopped, optional

★

SERVES 2

Grill tortillas and you have a quesadilla. Roll them and smother them with sauce and you have enchiladas. Deep-fry one and you have chips or a crunchy bowl for your fiesta salad at the hospital cafeteria. But if you pop a fresh tortilla in the oven and treat it with respect, you can bake up some crunchy, lo-cal wedges for scooping up a light fruit salsa perfectly suited for before-bed nibbling.

★ ★ ★

★ Preheat the oven to 400ºF. Line a baking sheet with aluminum foil or parchment paper.
★ Spread the tortillas on top.
★ Whisk the egg white with 1 tablespoon of water until it's slightly frothy. Brush the tortillas with the egg wash and sprinkle with the sugar and cinnamon and nuts, if using.
★ Using scissors, cut each tortilla into six wedges.
★ Bake until golden brown, 5 to 7 minutes.

Fruit Salsa

A fruit salsa is a sneaky way to meet your recommended daily allowance of fruit. So force yourself. It's a great accompaniment for spicy grilled fish or chicken, taming the meat's potency with a bit of acidity and sweetness. It's just as handy in the dessert department, creating a zesty sauce for angel food cake, vanilla ice cream, or these toasted crisps. Just for the record, you may not drain a can of fruit cocktail and say it can pinch hit here.

This recipe uses pears, but the fruit can also be mangoes, melons, bananas, pineapple, peaches, strawberries, or nearly anything else that's in season.

★ ★ ★

★ Once you've prepared the fruits, there's nothing more to do than combine the ingredients.

1 ripe pear, chopped

1 orange, peeled, sectioned, and diced

1 small apple, peeled and grated

1 kiwi, finely diced

¼ cup unsweetened coconut flakes, toasted

1 tablespoon chopped pistachios

1 tablespoon tequila

Juice of 1 lime

★

MAKES 2 GENEROUS SERVINGS

12:30 AM

Too
Darned Hot

The air conditioner is on the fritz. Or you're lying in bed with the attic fan blowing from the foot of the bed, its hot air as refreshing as the dog's panting breath, which is not a metaphor but a contributing factor.

What can you eat when it's this infernal, when it's the heat and it's *also* the humidity? The covers of the paperbacks are curled up as if to give their contents breathing room. The person clinging to the other edge of the bed can't offer you anything but a pinky of sticky contact. Is there no surcease? Is there no refreshment? Isn't there something to eat that might offer some relief?

Wait! There *was* that food show we saw in England one summer in which the highlight of the studio chef's program was "every sort of treat made with the summer's least expensive ingredient." After several suspense-building promotional teasers throughout the show, it turned out that the summer's big offering was ice. That's tap water put into a little tray and frozen. And what were our chef's recipes? Freezing a bottle of vodka in a block of ice, chipping ice for lemonade, mixing water with juice to create ice lollys, shaving ice to make a "stand" for a bowl of chilled soup. Ice: the possibilities are seemingly endless, but they're not.

We've collected hot-weather dishes from the world over for this sultry hour. Here are Mexican fruit-and-water coolers; iced gazpachos from Spain (with one alternative stopover in Japan); Italian ices reinvented in mini, ready-in-a-minute versions; as well as revivals of all-American classics, such as pineapple sherbet and state-fair lemon shake-ups. Time to chill out.

hot-weather dishes from the World over

4 lemons, washed well and cut into quarters

6 tablespoons sugar

2 glasses crushed or shaved ice

Small sprig of mint, optional

Water

★

SERVES 2

First, picture a glass of lemonade made with the powdery contents of a tiny envelope. Think of inhaling that dust, the cloying sweetness, and the pallid lemon taste. Now put that out of your mind. Imagine instead the sharp bite of fresh lemons, the pungent fragrance of lemon oil, and the puckering tartness just barely offset by a sugary sweetness. This is lemonade worthy of a blue ribbon.

★ ★ ★

★ Squeeze the juice from the lemons into a martini shaker or a large lidded jar (see sidebar). Drop each squeezed lemon into the container as well, along with the sugar, crushed ice, and mint, if desired. Add a splash or two of water.

★ Shake it, baby, shake it. You want the ice to bruise the lemon rinds and release the lemon oil; you want the lemons to rattle the ice; and you want to feel like you're doing some serious nighttime chemistry.

★ Taste the lemonade. Add more sugar or water according to your taste.

Juicier Lemons

Rolling a lemon under the pressure of your palm helps to release the fruit's juice. But a quick spell in the microwave can produce even more juice. Cut the lemon in half, place it in a small microwave-safe bowl, and zap it for a minute. Allow the lemon to cool, then insert a fork into the pulp and turn it while squeezing the lemon half.

Pink Lemonade: Instead of the mint sprig, drop a pair of ripe strawberries or a dozen raspberries into the shaker to lend their blush.

Limeade: Replace the lemons with limes. If you can find the smaller Key limes, with their subtle, more perfumed taste, you'll need 8 or 10, depending on their size. By no means attempt this with the contents of the plastic limes the grocery sells. A good rule of thumb is this: If a fruit or vegetable is not suitable for even a brief game of Mr. Potato Head, you may not use it for cooking.

Tomcat Collins: In case your late-night thoughts run in this direction, you can certainly augment the lemonade with a shot of vodka. Since it's late, let's call that a tomcat Collins.

On vacation along the Mayan Riviera, we subsisted on every sort of agua fresca, the simple-as-can-be, everyday cooler made of fresh fruit and bottled water, sold by vendors and restaurants up and down the coast.

Amid these puréed refreshments, one unusual drink was recommended by an affable waiter, something he called "Mayan Gatorade." Our collective Spanish couldn't decipher its contents: an elixir as green as Easter grass concocted from pineapple, cucumber, something resembling Swiss chard, and perhaps some other item entirely lost in translation. It bore no resemblance to its salty, sugary namesake. It was a taste of another civilization, something you'd need to acquire a taste for, as one does for Campari or Roquefort cheese or mackerel sushi. None of our attempts to re-create the drink have succeeded.

But here are four elemental elixirs, four "fresh waters," all complements of the melon family, which we did manage to re-create stateside. Any one of these will provide cooling refreshment in less than a few minutes. For a thinner consistency, simply increase the amount of cold water.

★ ★ ★

★ The directions for all the recipes below is simple: For 2 drinks, put the listed ingredients into a blender and purée until smooth.

Agua Fresca de Cantalupo

2 cups ripe cantaloupe chunks

½ cup cold water

Juice of 2 Key limes (or ½ regular lime)

3 to 4 ice cubes

No need to relegate the cantaloupe to the dieter's plate with the obligatory scoop of cottage cheese and the sprig of pallid grapes. Nor should you be put off by its name, which comes from the Italian (not the Mayan) for "wolf howl." Its high water and low sugar content (a whole melon has only half the sugar of most apples) whizzes into a sweetly perfumed cooler.

Agua Fresca de Melon Dulce

Whipping up a drink from a honeydew melon is like gathering zillions of honeysuckle blossoms and licking the single drop of fragrant liqueur that clings to each pistil—but with less field work. When choosing a honeydew, buy a sweet smelling, slightly soft melon that gives a nice hollow thump when you tap it. The fruit doesn't ripen further after it's plucked from the vine.

3 cups ripe honeydew chunks

½ cup cold water

4 mint leaves

3–4 ice cubes

Agua Fresca de Sandia

You should remove most of the watermelon's seeds, but once blended, the little chips will settle to the bottom of the glass, which is how this is served in Mexico; the ground-up seeds add their own distinctive flavor.

Think about slurping a cold slushy drink on the deck of the swim club your family joined when you were in junior high. Or think about slicing up the watermelon you hauled out to the park's picnic shelter during a sudden downpour at the family reunion. Combine these two impressions, and you're close to this most summery watermelon slurry.

3 cups ripe watermelon chunks

1 cup cold water

½ teaspoon salt

3–4 ice cubes

Agua Fresca de Pepino

You might prefer this juice poured through a sieve. After straining, you can add ice cubes and blend again to make it slushier.

As far as vegetables go, cucumbers are something of a nutritional letdown. Not a whole lot going on in the forty-five calories a medium cuke offers. But the flesh, which is mostly water, puréed with ice (which is mostly water), makes a doubly satisfying thirst-quencher.

1½ large cucumbers, peeled, seeded, and chopped into chunks

Juice of 1 lime

¼ cup sugar

3 cups cold water

3–4 ice cubes

Simple Tomato Gazpacho with Goat-cheese Croutons

1 small slice stale peasant or sourdough bread

2 large tomatoes, peeled, halved horizontally, and seeded (strain and save the juice)

1 tablespoon red wine vinegar

2 tablespoons water

½ red bell pepper, seeded and cut into quarters

½ English cucumber, peeled, seeded, and cut into quarters

¼ cup chopped red onion

1 small clove garlic, smashed

2 tablespoons extra virgin olive oil

Salt and freshly ground pepper

★

SERVES 2

2 slices peasant bread

2 tablespoons olive oil

2 ounces goat cheese

Freshly ground pepper

Pinch of paprika

True gazpacho is thickened with stale bread that has been soaked in water, wine, vinegar, or tomato juice. But authenticity is not the issue at this hour. Hasty and equally tasty, this soup is meant for summer's best tomatoes, and yet it can manage with canned whole tomatoes as well.

Just for fun, we've appended a quick recipe for goat-cheese croutons, which might remind you of those bread "fishes" your mom would break up and scatter on your tomato soup after Sunday school.

★ ★ ★

★ In a bowl, break the bread into bits and pour on the tomato juice from seeding (or add ½ cup bottled tomato juice), the vinegar, and water. Let the bread soak.

★ Combine the tomatoes in a food processor along with the bell pepper, cucumber, red onion, garlic, olive oil, salt, and pepper. Whiz the mixture just enough to make a coarsely chopped soup. If your machine has a "pulse" option, use several bursts rather than continuous puréeing.

★ Add the soaked bread bits and pulse again, trying to keep a bit of the texture.

★ Check for seasoning. Serve chilled by adding a few ice cubes to the soup.

Goat-cheese Croutons

★ Preheat the oven to 350°F or use a toaster oven.

★ Brush each slice of the peasant bread with olive oil and toast it until golden brown.

★ Spread goat cheese on the toasts and toast them for an additional 2 minutes.

★ Sprinkle with cracked pepper and paprika. Cut the toasts into little triangles.

Peachy-Keen Gazpacho

It may be hard to imagine the splendor of fragrant peaches paired with sun-ripened tomatoes, but trust us, one sip of this and it will become your staple soup the entire month of August, when both fruits fill the bowls and windowsills of your kitchen. Try all yellow tomatoes, try white peaches, try nectarines—the confluence of these two fruits balances sweetness with acidity and rewards you with a dish of pure sunshine even after the sun goes down.

★ ★ ★

★ Chop the peaches, tomatoes, bell pepper, onion, cucumber, and basil leaves separately; you want to keep their flavors distinct. If you use a food processor, do them one at a time and try not to pulverize the poor things. Add each ingredient to a large glass bowl with the Grand Marnier and olive oil.

★ The only real issue is getting everything as cold as possible, which can take a while. Refrigerate or use the freezer, stirring often, if you're feeling impatient.

★ Once the soup is chilled, add salt and black pepper to taste and the hot pepper sauce (be circumspect with the fire power).

2 large ripe peaches

2 large tomatoes,
seeded and juiced
(reserve the strained juice)

½ red or yellow bell pepper

1 small sweet onion

1 English cucumber, peeled
and seeded

6 basil leaves, chopped

1 tablespoon Grand Marnier

1 tablespoon olive oil

Salt and freshly
ground pepper

1 or more dashes of
favorite hot sauce

★

SERVES 4

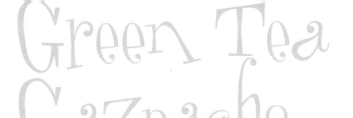

Green Tea Gazpacho

1 English cucumber, peeled
seeded, and cut into quarters

½ green bell pepper, seeded
and quartered

6 tomatillos, husked and
halved, or 1 green tomato,
halved and seeded

6 green tea bags
or 2 tablespoons
green tea leaves

1 cup boiling water

Juice of ½ lemon

Salt and freshly
ground pepper

Several dashes of green
Tabasco or favorite
hot sauce, optional

★

SERVES 2

The Far East meets Andalusia in this far-fetched, fragrant, and sublimely verdant soup. Served in small, clear glasses or bowls, this light gazpacho is dressy enough for a cocktail party but simple enough to sip in front of the window air conditioner on a sultry night.

★ ★ ★

★ In a food processor or blender, whiz together the cucumber, bell pepper, and tomatillos until smooth.

★ Brew the green tea in the boiling water. Steep for 2 to 3 minutes and strain it if you have used loose leaves. Add the lemon juice.

★ Pour the tea and vegetable purée into a glass bowl and add salt, pepper, and hot sauce, if using, to taste. If the mixture isn't cold enough, set the soup in the freezer for 10 minutes before serving.

Vermont Golden Apple Snow

Part zabaglione, part meringue, part apple pandowdy, part floating island: apple snow is nothing if not an anomaly. A frothy pudding. A bubbly mousse. If you want a novel late-night dessert, try this homespun favorite.

★ ★ ★

★ In a small saucepan, combine the maple syrup, heavy cream, and butter. Bring to a simmer and cook for about 10 minutes, or until the mixture thickens. Stir continuously, then set the pan aside to cool. You should have 1 cup of maple sauce.

★ Stir the spices into the strained applesauce.

★ With a small hand mixer, beat the egg whites in a dry bowl until they are frothy. Add the salt and continue beating the whites until soft peaks are formed.

★ Fold the egg whites into the applesauce by hand and then spoon the mixture into highball glasses.

★ Place the glasses in the refrigerator for an hour. When you're ready to chill out, drizzle the maple sauce on the apple snow and serve.

⅔ cup maple syrup

½ cup heavy cream

4 tablespoons unsalted butter

Pinch ground cinnamon

Pinch ground nutmeg

Pinch ground ginger

Pinch ground cloves

3 cups organic applesauce, strained to make 1½ cups coarse apple purée

2 large egg whites

Pinch of salt

★

SERVES 4

Freezer Pleezers

Your favorite fruits, cleaned, cut into pieces, and frozen, can metamorphose into fruit crèmes, sorbets, ices, granitas—whatever you'd like to call them as long as you don't resort to "sherbert," which, despite its nearly universal appearance on roadside menus, is nothing but a misspelling. The best part is these fruited ices can be served within minutes without your having to haul out that anniversary-present ice-cream maker you never remember to prefreeze (not that there's room in the freezer in the first place).

White Grape Sorbet

2 cups seedless white grapes, rinsed, removed from their stems, and frozen

½ cup confectioners' sugar, plus more for garnishing

1 tablespoon fresh lime juice

Small grape clusters for garnishing, optional

★

SERVES 2

Use this as the master recipe for creating the other flavors listed below. Try out your own variations, which could likewise prove fruitful. Each recipe will yield 2 servings. For making larger amounts, process more than one batch.

★ ★ ★

★ Combine the grapes, sugar, and lime juice in a food processor and pulse several times. Then blend continuously until the mixture forms an icy mass. Don't overdo it or you'll create more of a slurry.

★ Scoop the sorbet into cold martini glasses. Okay, a cereal bowl will do if it's only you.

★ For festive moments, go for the garnish: nestle a bundle of fresh grapes atop the sorbet and dust them with confectioners' sugar (just sprinkle on a pinch with your fingertips).

Banana/Strawberry Sorbet

A banana presents so many healthy opportunities—to say nothing of its overripened role in banana-nut bread—no wonder it's sold in bunches. Throw one in the blender for this icy delight, and then create a hand moisturizer by mashing a banana with a little butter; create an exfoliating mask by blending a banana with white clay; shampoo your hair with a ripe banana mixed with almond oil; or place banana slices on any area of dry skin and let the oils and vitamins sink in for 20 minutes.

1 banana, peeled and frozen

1 cup strawberries, frozen

Juice of ½ lime

Pineapple Rum Sorbet

This sorbet hints of a swim-up bar at a resort in the Bahamas. It recalls the Polynesian restaurant with the smoking drinks and the souvenir tikki god tumblers where your grandparents took you for your tenth birthday. But despite all this, it's pretty darned tasty.

1 cup fresh pineapple chunks, frozen

2 tablespoons Myers's Dark Rum

Toasted coconut shards, optional, for garnishing

¼ cup coconut milk, optional, for more of a piña colada taste

Apricot Blizzard

We know you're skeptical. We know you're wondering how can we offer, after so many highbrow suggestions, a dessert that merely involves a can of fruit. But here, the cloyingly sweet syrup and the otherwise all-too-mushy fruit are redeemed in this easy-freeze-and-frappé method. For once, convenience needn't be mocked.

One 14-ounce can apricots in syrup, emptied into a plastic bag and frozen

Juice of 1 lemon

Rasperry Ice Cream

2 cups frozen raspberries in sugar syrup, or 2 cups dry-pack frozen raspberries plus ½ cup confectioners' sugar

1 cup heavy cream, chilled

1 teaspoon Grand Marnier, optional

VARIATIONS

You can substitute other frozen fruits for this ice cream, such as peaches, assorted berries, or cherries.

Fresh raspberries are as heavenly scented as old-fashioned roses, and freezing them to death in simple syrup kills most of that aroma. So unless you have an overabundance of raspberries in your garden (and the chance to sugar and freeze them ahead of time), use a package of previously frozen berries, which are already suited for this chilling experience.

Banana Ice Cream

2 ripe bananas, peeled and frozen in pieces

½ cup heavy cream

2 teaspoons lemon juice

1 teaspoon vanilla extract

2 tablespoons black walnuts, chopped, optional

Whenever we bring a banana into the dessert arena, we can't help but recall one of Elvis's legendary midnight snacks: a single banana sautéed in a stick of butter. Even with the heavy cream, this dessert doesn't quite pack the fat wallop of Elvis's beddie-bye boost.

★ Combine and blend the ingredients as directed in the sorbet master recipe on page 104.

★ Fold the walnuts, if using, into the ice cream after it leaves the food processor.

VARIATIONS

To transform this ice cream into a mock banana split, drizzle the banana ice cream with chocolate sauce, spoon on strawberry and pineapple sauces, and dot with chopped peanuts.

Freezing Fruits

With almost no preparation, fresh fruits can be frozen for use in ice creams and smoothies without losing much in the way of flavor or texture. In each case, prepare the fruits as directed below. Remove as much air as possible from the plastic bags after filling, to minimize frost. Most fruit will survive a several-month cryogenic trip to the center of the freezer and back.

Bananas: If you can see that you'll never finish the whole bunch of bananas you've purchased, peel any ripe fruit, break it into a couple of pieces, and bag and freeze the chunks. Hard bananas whose skins have not spotted are too starchy for this purpose.

Berries: Place fresh berries on a baking sheet in a single layer and slide the tray into the freezer for several hours. Pour the frozen berries into plastic bags and return them to the freezer.

Grapes: Rinse the fruit, remove the stems, place them in a bag, and freeze them.

Melons, papayas, pineapple: Peel the fruit, remove the seeds or core, and cut the fruit into 2-inch pieces. Bag and freeze.

Stone fruits (peaches, plums, apricots): Remove the pits, quarter the fruit, and freeze the pieces in bags. If you prefer the fruits peeled, feel free. Mangoes can be frozen similarly, but they do require peeling.

crumbs in Bed

You're awakened by a thunderstorm's cracking and the dog digging to get under the covers, or you're waiting up to fold the last load of clothes still spinning in the dryer. You need something to eat, but nothing that requires silverware or even a plate—just a napkin to wipe your fingers.

Or maybe you're up with your husband, who's marking his fifth grader's attempts at a "persuasive letter" or studying for his law-school entrance exam. You're happy to keep him company, watching the first of four *Dynamic Public Speaking* videos your company purchased in lieu of sending you to the conference in Key West; the volume's turned to a whisper, and you're sitting on your pillow two feet from the set. You both need something to munch on while your night shifts continue, if only to offer each other solidarity with contrapuntal crunching.

To inspire, or at least distract, you (whether that's "you" in the singular, eating alone, or "you" in the plural, gathered around the kitchen table), we've created several resourceful concoctions of grains, nuts, berries, crisps, toasted grains, and seasonings. While we do offer you an opportunity to shop for a few items you might not stock in your pantry, most of these crunchy mixtures can be made with even a relatively bare cupboard. They're all substantial improvements over microwaved popcorn or boxes of Junior Mints. They're big bowls of little bits, for that hand-to-bowl-to-mouth cycle that's strangely placating at this hour.

big bowls of little bits

Parmesan Popcorn

¼ cup freshly grated
Parmesan cheese (use the
finest holes on your grater)

¼ teaspoon turmeric

½ teaspoon paprika

One 3-ounce bag unsalted
microwave popcorn, freshly
popped (14 to 15 cups)

★

SERVES 2

For this book we stayed up night after night sampling snacks from dozens of friends who offered to share their furtive before-bed bites. We tested a plethora of peanut-butter-and-banana arrangements, dipped and dredged crackers though dozens of spreads, and witnessed umpteen forms of culinary torture visited upon unsuspecting pantry items.

And we have to admit we liked too many of these jury-rigged foods. In particular, we were surprised at our friend Peter's cheesy orange popcorn, the color of, well, boxed macaroni and cheese. We asked, how did it get that way? "Just sprinkle a couple table-spoons of that dried-cheese powder from the envelope right into the bag of popcorn as soon as it's done popping. Shake it. Eat it." In our version we added melted butter, but then we didn't feel you needed a recipe for that.

It inspired us, however, to find a way for pretentious foodies (like us), who don't have a box of macaroni and cheese on hand, to create this utterly orange and cheesy nosh. You can use microwaved popcorn, air-popped corn, or any other hot popped kernels. What you can't use is the elbow macaroni.

★ ★ ★

★ In a small bowl, mix together the cheese, turmeric,
and paprika.

★ Open the bag of freshly
popped popcorn and sprinkle on
the seasoned cheese. Close the
bag, shake, shake, shake, and
then give it a try.

Gonzo Garbanzos

We have been defeated by our pledge to banish the deep-fryer from the night owl's kitchen. But convincing arguments were made that these blissful bites were not meant to be made at midnight, merely consumed then. Or anytime. So we relented. This once.

The chickpea, as Mike Myers (in his guise as Linda Richmond) taught us, is neither a chick nor a pea—discuss. Indeed, this peculiar legume may be the first thing kids fish out of their salads, but it has a noble reputation: it's used for treating snakebites, warts, sunstroke, bronchitis, and lowering cholesterol. And it has three culinary claims to fame: falafel, hummus, and now this snack, which turns a can of ever-ready garbanzo beans into the antithesis of their squishy tinned selves. Like roasted soybeans or giant hominy kernels, these peas are a snappy—and fiery—nibble for solo munching or for combining with other crackers, stix, nuts, and mixes.

★ ★ ★

One 14-ounce can garbanzo beans (chickpeas)

Peanut or vegetable oil for deep-frying

1 teaspoon sea salt

1 teaspoon paprika

½ teaspoon cayenne pepper

★

MAKES 2 CUPS

★ Open and drain the chickpeas in a colander. Run cold water over the chickpeas to remove any of the viscous goo clinging from the can. Drain the peas on a tea towel and gently roll them to soak up the surface water.

★ In a deep-fryer or medium, heavy-gauge saucepan, heat the oil to 350°F. In a medium bowl, mix together the salt, paprika, and cayenne pepper. Set aside.

★ Fry the peas in several batches until they are golden brown. Allow the peas to drain on paper towels; while they are still warm, toss the peas with the seasoning mixture.

★ Serve these nutty bits while they're warm. Once the chickpeas have cooled completely, they will hold for a couple of days in an airtight container.

Hot and Sweet Pumpkin-Seed Brittle

4 tablespoons unsalted butter

½ cup packed light
brown sugar

2 tablespoons light
corn syrup

½ teaspoon cayenne pepper

2 cups hulled pumpkin seeds,
roasted (see Note page 113)

1 cup pine nuts

★

MAKES JUST UNDER
1 POUND

A plucky switch from the peanut brittle you find on your mother-in-law's platter of Christmas cookies, this brittle abounds with a buttery taste provided by the seeds themselves, which we simply emphasize with some real butter. And because you use hulled pumpkin seeds rather than the seeds you scoop out of the jack-o'-lantern, there's no reason to limit this treat to the fall months.

One recipe creates a bounty of brittle. While you can certainly cut the specified quantities in half, this treat is so overwhelmingly enticing, you'll find yourself proving one of our Laws of Culinary Physics: It takes no longer for a large batch to disappear than it does a small batch.

★ Line a jelly-roll pan with aluminum foil and butter the foil.

★ Combine the butter, brown sugar, corn syrup, and cayenne in a medium, heavy-gauge saucepan. Place the pan over medium heat and stir everything together.

★ Once the butter has melted and incorporated the sugar and syrup, add the pumpkin seeds and pine nuts. Continue to stir and raise the heat to medium-high. The seeds and nuts will become toasty brown in color and the mixture will begin to thicken and turn amber. This should take 5 minutes.

* Dump the mixture onto the jelly-roll pan and smooth the surface with the back of a spoon. Press the brittle to create as thin a layer as possible.
* Cool the brittle and then break it into pieces, peeling the foil away. Store the brittle in an airtight container.

NOTE: Hulled, roasted pumpkin seeds are available at health food stores and larger groceries.

Checkered Mixes

1 cup walnut halves

1 cup whole almonds

10 grissini (thin bread sticks),
broken into 2-inch pieces

1 cup plain whole wheat
Melba rounds

2 tablespoons extra virgin
olive oil

1 tablespoon chopped
fresh rosemary, or
2 teaspoons dried

2 cloves garlic, finely minced

Juice of ½ lemon

1 teaspoon sea salt

Freshly ground pepper

2 tablespoons freshly grated
Parmesan cheese

★

MAKES 4 CUPS

We think of these hard-working nuts and berries and chips and bits as night kitchen kibble. Though humble, they're hardly humdrum. Our hope is that you'll join with us and renounce all packaged snackage—even if they're now available in your favorite flavors: dried-up chive, dehydrated liquid smoke, garlic-powdered salt, etc.

All of the following innovative mixes can be served while warm—slightly cooled after baking—or stored, when completely cooled, in an airtight container.

Everything's Coming Up Tuscan Mix

★ Preheat the oven to 250°F.

★ Combine the walnuts, almonds, grissini, and Melba rounds in a large mixing bowl.

★ In a small bowl, mix together the olive oil, rosemary, garlic, and lemon juice. Pour this over the dry mix and toss well. Sprinkle with the salt and pepper.

★ Spread the mixture on a baking sheet and bake for 35 to 40 minutes, tossing occasionally. Remove the sheet from the oven and cool the mix slightly before dusting it with the Parmesan.

South of the Border Mix-Up

★ Preheat the oven to 250°F.

★ Combine the corn cereal, cashew pieces, and tortilla pieces in a large mixing bowl.

★ In a small bowl, mix together the vegetable oil, lime juice, garlic cloves, hot sauce, chili powder, cumin, oregano, cayenne pepper, and salt. Pour this over the dry mix and toss to coat everything evenly.

★ Spread the mixture on a baking sheet and bake for 35 to 40 minutes, tossing occasionally.

1 cup puffed corn cereal

1 cup toasted corn cereal, such as Corn Chex

1 cup unsalted roasted cashew pieces

2 flour tortillas, cut into 1-inch pieces

3 tablespoons vegetable oil

2 tablespoons fresh lime juice

2 cloves garlic, finely minced

4 dashes of hot sauce

1 teaspoon chili powder

½ teaspoon ground cumin

½ teaspoon dried oregano

Pinch or more cayenne pepper

1 teaspoon salt

★

MAKES 3½ CUPS

Buffalo Wingnuts

1 cup unsalted roasted peanuts

1 cup pretzel fish crackers (or other small pretzel bits)

1 cup puffed wheat cereal

1 cup toasted wheat cereal, such as Wheat Chex

4 tablespoons (½ stick) unsalted butter

¼ cup favorite hot sauce

1 tablespoon white vinegar

1 tablespoon Worcestershire sauce

★

MAKES 4 CUPS

★ Preheat the oven to 250°F.

★ Combine the peanuts, pretzels, and wheat cereals in a large mixing bowl.

★ In a glass measuring cup, mix together the butter, hot sauce, white vinegar, and Worcestershire sauce and zap for 1 minute in the microwave. Pour the heated mixture over the dry mix and toss to coat evenly.

★ Spread the mixture on a baking sheet and bake for 35 to 40 minutes, tossing occasionally.

Easy Pecan-ese Mix

Our favorite of the bunch, this grouping is more au natural, with just an extra teasing of spices on the coated pecans. Of course, the spiced pecans run the danger of never making it into the mix—they're that tempting. We also serve them with cocktails, all by themselves. Those and a couple of martini olives, and guests often don't need more than a simple salad.

★ Combine all the ingredients in a large bowl and toss.

2 cups Twice-Spiced Pecans, cooled (see below)

1 cup dried sour cherries or dried cranberries

1 cup salted roasted pumpkin seeds

½ cup sunflower seeds

½ cup golden raisins

½ cup sesame sticks

½ cup dried apricots

★

MAKES 6 CUPS

Twice-Spiced Pecans

★ Preheat the oven to 300°.
★ Combine everything but the pecans in a glass measuring cup. Zap the mixture in the microwave for 1 minute.
★ Place the pecans in a medium bowl and pour the melted butter mixture (unsalted butter, balsamic vinegar, granulated or brown sugar, hot sauce, cumin, rosemary, cayenne pepper, and salt) over them.
★ Spread the coated pecans on a baking sheet and bake for 10 to 15 minutes, until golden. Toss the pecans during the baking process to separate them a bit. Let them cool completely before sealing them in—what else?—an airtight container.

2 tablespoons unsalted butter

1 teaspoon balsamic vinegar

1 tablespoon granulated or brown sugar

2 dashes of favorite hot sauce

1 teaspoon ground cumin

2 teaspoons dried rosemary, or 1 tablespoon minced fresh

½ teaspoon cayenne pepper

½ teaspoon salt

Freshly ground pepper

2 cups pecan halves

★

MAKES 2 CUPS

1:00 AM

Spa Night

Let's say you're up transferring your favorite Motown records to CDs now that two hours of tech support has figured out why the software keeps crashing. Or you're blurry from surfing the Internet for cheap, off-the-beaten-path, private casitas for your February vacation in Costa Rica (time-saving clue: there are none). You're sorting through your closet and end up covering the bed with *unworn* clothes you thought you'd never live without. And let's say you didn't have the luxury of spending the afternoon at a day spa. It's one in the morning, and what you need is a night spa. Even an hour's worth.

Merely soaking in a tub with a bubble bath is enough to relax most tense muscles, open up the skin's pores, encourage greater circulation, and cause the pages of your magazine to stick together. But there's always that tension fretting over which aromatherapy component to add to the bath. What essential oil will coax you into that much-needed state of repose: every phial claims something that sounds exactly the same. Do you want vetiver to "soothe your state of mental exhaustion," or lavender to "calm your anxiousness"? Tea tree oil, sandalwood, orange, cypress, chamomile, ylang-ylang: they all pledge to alleviate tension, flood your senses with peacefulness, absolve you of worries, nurture your sense of well-being, restore your inner balance, balance your checkbook, renew your library books, and find that special something for the man in your life. Where, oh where, is *the* one that says "will put you out like a light"?

We think every spa treatment worth its weight in Epsom salts includes a little nourishment as well. Here are light, enlightening foods to bask in, to imbibe, and to plaster on your face in a scary spackling of orange or green goo. From India we've brought you yogurt potions. From Japan we've found a crystal-clear elixir your whole body can absorb from the inside and the outside. We've gathered up such incandescent indulgences as green teas, tropical fruits, avocado oils, and papaya purée with its enzymatic wizardry. And with a range of midnight misos, we've set out a soup that brings a millennium of tradition to your nightstand.

If you don't indulge yourself, who will? Come on: Draw the bath. Put on the tea kettle. Start the blender screeching. You deserve it.

Japanese Sake Bath

4 cups inexpensive sake

4 ounces expensive sake

★

SERVES 1

This exotic, serene restorative is found in ancient Japanese traditions. You both bathe in and imbibe the same ingredient: sake, the divine, clear wine made from distilled rice. Sake in the bathwater softens and cleanses the skin, while sake in your mouth does something a bit more spiritual.

By the way, don't mind the dingy color of the bathwater after your soak: sake also draws toxins from the skin. Who knew that about sake? Who knew that about skin*?*

★ ★ ★

★ In keeping with the ceremony of Japanese bathing, shower as the tub fills with the warm, inviting water.

★ Pour the inexpensive sake into the filled bathtub and stir.

★ Pour yourself the smaller amount of fine sake and slide into the tub. Poach yourself for a minimum of 30 minutes, until you're radiating both inside and out. One note of caution: The alcohol, as well as the water's heat, will give you a flush sensation. Take your time rising from the tub. Nothing spoils a calm radiance like slipping on the bath mat.

Three Facial Frappés

If truth be told (and decidedly we have not told the good people at Broadway Books), drinking water is probably the only thing you ought to be consuming at this hour. It is the universal solvent, after all, and you probably are still shy of the eight glasses you were supposed to guzzle during the day. But let's leave that aside for the moment; need and want so rarely align.

Sure, it's possible to rejuvenate your skin with any number of tony cosmetics, but how many can you apply and then drink? Blend a batch of these fruited tonics and then . . . it's drench your skin with one half and it's down the hatch with the other.

★ ★ ★

Tropical Mask and Milkshake

The yogurt's enzymes soften and whiten the skin. The papaya exfoliates and applies a vitamin E poultice. The lemon and kiwi provide vitamin C, which promises to reduce surface wrinkles and protect skin cells from free-radical damage.

But does this really work? you ask. How can you know if anything really works? You get a friend to try it. Barring that, you try it yourself for several months and decide. Worst case, you've enjoyed several months of a delicious frozen shake and spent a few hours with papaya on your face.

★ ★ ★

★ Blend the yogurt, lemon, 1 kiwi, and ½ papaya.

★ Remove half of the mixture to use for the mask. Smooth the cream over your face or any dry area of skin. Leave it on for 15 minutes.

★ To make the smoothie, combine the remaining fruit and the frozen yogurt in the blender jar with the remaining purée. Blend until smooth and then drink up while the mask dries. (Wash off the mask with warm water and wipe clean with a towel.)

1 cup plain yogurt

½ lemon, peeled and seeded

2 kiwis, peeled

1 papaya, peeled and seeded

½ cup vanilla nonfat frozen yogurt

★

SERVES 1

Avocado Mask and Dip

1 avocado, pitted, peeled, and cut into pieces

1 tablespoon lime juice

2 tablespoons chopped onion

Salt and freshly ground pepper

Assorted fresh vegetable sticks and/or corn chips

Avocados not only are great moisturizers but are full of vitamin E and healthy mono-unsaturated fats (the kind your doctor wants you to consume). One of nature's perfect foods, avocados should be on everyone's list of top five foods to have if stranded on a desert island—if only because there's not going to be much else growing there.

- Purée the avocado and lime juice in a blender or food processor. Remove half of the mixture and smooth it over your face or any dry skin. Leave it on for 15 minutes.
- To make the dip, add the chopped onion to the remaining avocado purée and season with salt and pepper.
- Dip to your heart's content while the mask dries. Visualization helps: picture yourself on the beach in Acapulco, basking among the palms and the ogling tourists with ill-considered bathing suits. Feeling better already?
- Wash off the mask with warm water and wipe clean with a towel.

English Cucumber Facial and Frappé

Cukes are cool and calming. Pineapples are exfoliating and brash. Yogurt is whitening and soothing. Mint is invasive and nearly impossible to rid yourself of once you've stupidly planted it in your yard. Together, these make a civilized refreshment.

★ Cut two slices from the cucumber and set them aside: these are your eye patches. Seed the remaining cucumber. Cut it into chunks and combine it with the pineapple and yogurt in a food processor or a blender.

★ Purée and then remove half of the mixture for the mask.

★ Add a few ice cubes, the mint, and the lemon juice to the blender's remaining liquid. Blend until you've made a frothy liquid.

★ Apply the mask and then, before placing the cucumber slices over your eyes, grab the smoothie and sip.

★ Leave the mask on for 15 minutes, then wash it off with warm water and wipe clean with a towel.

1 cucumber, peeled and seeded

1 cup fresh or home-frozen pineapple chunks (not canned)

1 cup plain nonfat yogurt

1 teaspoon chopped mint, or a pinch of dried

Juice of ½ lemon

Green Tea-for-Two Smoothie

1½ cups soy milk

4 green tea bags

4 kiwis, peeled or unpeeled

**1 banana, peeled and broken
into pieces**

1 tablespoon honey

Ice cubes

★

SERVES 2

Doubly green from both kiwis and green tea, this smoothie must have the power to turn back the hands of time—or at least thumb-wrestle with them until they cry "uncle." The kiwi skins are edible, adding, as you must have guessed, a bit more fiber, as well as their own earthier flavor. Try including them one time; not having to scoop out the kiwi flesh saves some time, too.

★ ★ ★

★ In a saucepan or a microwave-safe bowl, bring the soy milk just to the point of simmering.

★ Steep the tea bags in the milk for 5 minutes, then pour the liquid into a blender. Discard the tea bags or dry them, spray-paint them silver, and hang them on your Christmas tree. They're Mrs. Claus's clutch purses.

★ Add the fruit pieces and honey, along with a few ice cubes. Blend until smooth.

The Green-Teaing of America

All tea—green, black, and oolong—comes from the leaves of the same shrub, *Camellia sinensis*. Plucked by hand year-round (only the bud and the first two leaves are used in the best teas), this plant has inspired some 3,000 varieties of tea.

In making green tea, the leaves are picked, allowed to wilt briefly, and then immediately steamed, baked, or pan-heated. No fermentation (oxidization) occurs, as it does in the processing of black and oolong tea. Green tea is the reigning preference in China and Japan. Curiously, it used to be England's most popular tea until the eighteenth century. Even customers in the United States preferred green tea to black until about 1915. Indeed, most of the tea thrown overboard during the Boston Tea Party happened to be green tea.

One variety you might consider for late-night drinking is gen-mai cha, which contains sencha (green) tea with roasted grains of rice. All green teas contain less caffeine than black teas, and in a typical cup of gen-mai cha there is even less tea because the rice provides half the flavor. The result is a satisfying cup with minimal caffeine content.

Jasmine teas, as well as the rarer "white" teas (for which the buds and leaves are steamed just after picking rather than dried or cured, thereby conferring no grassy or smoky undertones), are also particularly relaxing at night. Once again, if you are especially sensitive to caffeine, be vigilant: look for decaffeinated varieties.

**1 cup plain nonfat
or low-fat yogurt**

1 cup skim milk

**1 tablespoon honey or
maple syrup**

★

SERVES 2

Throughout the Middle East and Eastern Asia, yogurt is an essential drink. Each country has its own original versions: Some are thinner or more dilute, served as a beverage with a meal. Others are thicker and more substantial, served as a light meal in and of themselves. Some concoctions are fruity sweet, while others are savory, blended with cumin, salt, ginger, or other regional spices. Still others are as sophisticated as the fragrance of roses—which is because they're actually scented with rose water or garnished with fresh petals.

Of course, indigenous yogurts are typically anything but low-fat (which does count for some of their appeal), but we have specified lighter versions for the middle of the night. And don't forget: Lassi is probiotic! Active yogurt cultures are doing your body good.

★ ★ ★

★ Combine the ingredients in a blender and let 'er rip. Pour the frothy liquid over a glass of ice.

VARIATIONS

Lemon Lassi: Add the grated zest of 1 lemon. For more lemon power, add 1 drop of lemon extract. (Don't be tempted to add lemon juice, which will make the yogurt curdle.)

Indian Spice Lassi: Add a pinch of ground cardamom, ginger, cumin, and black pepper.

Pistachio and Honey Lassi: Blend in ½ cup of pistachios and one more tablespoon of honey.

Honeydew and Ginger Lassi: Add 1 cup of honeydew cubes and ½ teaspoon ground ginger (or a nickel-size coin of fresh ginger).

Mint or Persian Lassi: Add 10 fresh mint leaves.

Other Fruit Lassis: If you're in the mood for something pink, add ½ cup of strawberries, raspberries, or cherries. In a blue mood, go with blueberries or blackberries. Any ripe fruit—about ½ cup—can be added to the basic lassi. Mango lassi is an Indian favorite.

**1½ cups dashi (seaweed
stock) or vegetable or
chicken broth**

Pinch of sugar

Dash of soy sauce

Dash of sake, optional

**4 shiitake mushrooms
(or other fresh mushrooms),
cleaned and sliced**

1 tablespoon miso

2 tablespoons diced tofu

**1 tablespoon slivered
scallions**

★

SERVES 1

Called "meat from the fields" in Japan, soybeans have been a staple of that nation for thousands of years. In this nation, the erstwhile unappreciated soybean has become something of an overachiever in just the last decade: grocery stores are replete with soy sauce, miso, roasted soybeans, edamame, tofu, soy frozen desserts, soy milk, soy cheese, protein powder, soy burgers, soy bacon—soy vey is all we can say in our best Yiddish.

Miso, the fermented paste of soybeans (or rice or wheat), is crammed with flavor, protein, fat, and so many nutrients that you'd think miso alone could keep a person healthy, wealthy, and wise.

The principle behind this soup? Allow the fragrant stock base to provide a flavorful broth for a flash-cooking of spare ingredients—a balance of herbs, greens, vegetables, and perhaps a bit of meat. And just as each region of Japan is known for its own miso, this soup is amazingly adaptable to the wants and shortcomings of a late-night kitchen.

A Few Facts About Miso

Since miso will keep for months in the refrigerator, and since you use only a small amount each time, you're destined to find a range of uses for the intense paste. Beyond soups, miso can feature in salad dressings, as spreads for sandwiches, as flavor enhancements in stews or sauces, or in rubs and marinades for fish and meats.

The best and freshest miso does not contain MSG. There are many varieties typically available at Asian groceries, health food stores, and large food emporia, as well as more unusual artisanal misos with other additions, such as chickpeas or dandelion greens. In Japan, miso is so varied and customized, it's a signature of each region. For starters, it's enough just to know the three basic types: Soy miso has a bolder flavor, thick consistency, and assertive saltiness. White or light miso is a relatively sweet concentrate made from rice. And red miso is made from barley, and is darker in color and in flavor.

★ ★ ★

- ★ In a glass measuring cup or earthenware mug, combine the dashi, sugar, soy sauce, sake, if using, and mushrooms. Cover with plastic wrap and microwave for 2 minutes. Allow the broth to steep for 5 minutes.
- ★ Stir the miso into the broth and add the tofu. If the liquid isn't hot enough, return the cup to the microwave for an additional 30 seconds, but don't allow the liquid to boil, since that kills the fragrance and the beneficial flora of the miso.
- ★ Add the scallions and serve.

SEASONAL ADDITIONS

Part of what makes traditional miso soup sublime is the selection and balance of individual ingredients. More is not merrier in this case. Choose among these suggestions or try your own inventions, remembering that restraint is the order of the day—er, night.

- ★ Chopped greens, such as spinach, tatsoi, or arugula (added when the miso is stirred in)
- ★ Slivers of fennel, bok choy, broccoli, zucchini, asparagus tips, or sugar snap peas (added initially, before the first heating)
- ★ A few strips of salmon or chicken (if uncooked, add at the start of the recipe and allow the meat to be poached; if cooked, add along with the miso)
- ★ Rice noodles, cooked rice, bean sprouts (added along with the tofu)
- ★ Small bits of dried seaweed (added at the start of the recipe)

1:15 AM

under the covers

You've raided the refrigerator . . . You've opened every one of Mother Hubbard's cupboards and found them bare. You meant to go shopping on the way home. Moreover, you've been saying that for a week. There's no inspiration in limp celery, a can of tomato paste, grapefruits from your sister's trip to Florida, and a gift assortment of teas named with verbs like "Actualize" and "Transcend" instead of flavors.

You've read the back of the instant pudding box for the second time in a week, debating whether or not it's worth drinking the pudding since you don't plan to be up when it gets around to thickening.

So there's nothing to do but head to bed and call it a wrap—which is the whole idea of this chapter.

When fresh ingredients are limited and the larder's this bare, it's time to use the improv skills you honed in drama club when you played paperbag dramatics. Remember? That's where the teacher puts whatever unlikely objects she can gather up into a sack, and you and your teammates have to incorporate everything into a quick skit. So, you didn't grow up to be a thespian, it's still a strategy that works for these easy, everyday wrappers.

One suggestion involves lettuce, another utilizes sandwich bread—two items stocked in even the barest households—while our third recipe features an item you ought to consider stocking: Vietnamese rice papers. This light, fat-free, nearly calorie-free wrapper "cooks" in a few seconds of warm water, bundles up a wide array of offerings and leftovers, and, thereby, distinguishes itself as the ideal tool of impatient late-night snackers.

Are you ready to roll?

head to bed and call it a wrap

1 small head Boston lettuce, leaves separated and cleaned

1 seared tuna steak, thinly sliced, or one 4-ounce can tuna fish, drained

6 Niçoise or other pitted olives (forget those pitted, pitiful canned black ones that taste like brined Styrofoam)

½ cup peeled and diced English cucumber (or leftover steamed beans, sugar peas, or fennel)

1 small tomato, diced

2 tablespoons chopped flat-leaf parsley

1 small spoonful of capers

1 hard-boiled egg, chopped, optional

1 cup cooked rice, optional

2 tablespoons olive oil

2 tablespoons fresh lemon juice

Freshly ground pepper

One o'clock at night is hardly the time to trot out the salad spinner. But for late-night snacking, a single ample lettuce leaf can make an ideal "plate" or wrapper, providing the conveyance for an array of sandwich-like trappings.

Now, if you can predict a late evening ahead, a bit of earlier preparation will reward you with even tastier fare. Simply sear or grill a piece of fresh tuna or a small beef filet and refrigerate it for the evening's snack.

★ ★ ★

★ Place two whole lettuce leaves on a work surface and chop the remaining leaves.
★ Divide the chopped lettuce, tuna, olives, cucumber, tomato, parsley, and capers between the leaves. If you are famished, add the egg and rice.
★ Swirl together the oil, lemon juice, and pepper and drizzle over the salad.
★ You can roll up the large outer leaf into a tube and munch the salad as you would a burrito, or bring out the knife and fork.

VARIATIONS

Instead of bagels, bread, tortillas, or other carb-rich conveyances, consider using lettuce leaves to package these salads and fillings:

★ Romaine lettuce "roll-up" with a chopped Caesar salad
★ Lettuce rolls of Cobb salad
★ Roast beef, Stilton cheese, and horseradish sauce sheathed in radicchio (use a favorite horseradish sauce or concoct one with equal parts plain yogurt or mayonnaise and pure grated horseradish)
★ Be adventurous: use lettuce leaves to wrap up a few tablespoons of leftover fried rice or other Chinese carryout, cold pasta salad, grilled vegetables, a scoop of chutney with goat cheese or other semisoft cheese

Dressing Up

While there's always the stand of bedraggled bottled dressings in the fridge door, in a matter of minutes you can whip up a jar of dressing versatile enough to welcome any number of zesty fillips.

CLASSIC VINAIGRETTE

★ Combine all the ingredients and whisk to incorporate. Store in a sealed jar in the refrigerator.

VARIATIONS

Blue Cheese Vinaigrette: For a steak salad, substituting beef for the tuna in the Salade Niçoise, go for this creamy, robust vinaigrette. Substitute an equal amount of champagne vinegar for the other two vinegars and add ⅓ cup crumbled blue cheese when you whisk up the ingredients.

Black Pepper Citronette:
If you replace the tuna in Salade Niçoise with roasted or smoked chicken, try this tart dressing. Use fresh lemon juice in place of the vinegars. Double the amount of black pepper. Omit the thyme. Add ¼ cup freshly grated Parmigiano-Reggiano cheese. Whisk as before.

½ **extra virgin olive oil (here, the quality of the olive oil counts for something)**

2 tablespoons **balsamic vinegar**

2 tablespoons red wine **vinegar**

1 small shallot, minced

2 teaspoons Dijon mustard

1 teaspoon chopped fresh **thyme, or a pinch of dried**

½ **teaspoon freshly ground pepper**

½ **teaspoon sea salt**

★

MAKES 1 CUP

Rice Paper Rolls

Two 8-inch rice paper wrappers

Your choice of fillings (list follows)

2 Boston lettuce leaves, optional

Your choice of dipping sauces (recipes follow)

★

MAKES 2 ROLLS

We love Vietnamese rice papers and all the fillings they obligingly enrobe. Rice paper rolls are the least fussy of any wrap: they're ready in seconds, and they're nearly imperishable (you can keep an opened package on your shelf for months). And did we say inexpensive? Softened and stuffed, they're ready to dip in a matter of moments. The only trick is the little business of rolling them, which takes just a bit of practice; the dampened rice paper feels like thin silk and needs to be treated carefully. If the first few tear, who cares? It's midnight, after all, and there are still plenty more wrappers in the package for practicing.

Here are a few combinations, as well as three quick dipping sauces.

★ ★ ★

★ Submerge a rice wrapper in a shallow bowl of warm water for 30 seconds or until it's just pliable. The sheet will continue to "cook," so pull it from the bath before it's entirely limp. Set the wet wrapper on a clean, dry towel.

★ Place a small handful of the filling mixture in the center of the disk. Holding the edge of the wrapper closest to you, fold the wrapper over the filling and tuck it under. Fold in the two sides and then roll the filled portion over the remainder of the wrapper, sealing the package completely.

★ Place each finished roll inside a leaf of lettuce to add an extra layer of crunch and support. Serve with a dipping sauce.

FULFILLING FILLINGS

★ For a bright green snap, try to include whole herb sprigs, such as cilantro, mint, or basil. Add shredded salad greens, spinach, cabbage, or scallions.

★ For crunch, drop in a julienne of cucumber, jicama, carrots, and perhaps some cooked rice noodles or bean thread noodles. Water chestnuts, roasted soybeans, and peanuts are great as well.

★ Other vegetables can contribute their own singular character: mushrooms, bok choy, asparagus, radishes, avocados, grilled eggplant, or zucchini, etc.

- Add a squeeze of lime juice and a squirt of sesame or hot chili oil to the mixture before wrapping.
- Your fridge might hold any number of suitable meats to augment the packages, such as poached or roasted chicken breast, thinly sliced flank steak, or chopped cooked shrimp or crabmeat.

DIPPING SAUCES

If we were to draw a map of your tongue highlighting the various tasting zones, each of these dips would careen among the salty, sour, and sweet spots on the road trip of your mouth. To create any of these dips, whisk together the listed ingredients in a small bowl.

Tangy Lime Dipping Sauce

The tangy lime sauce has a pungent citrus note, a salinity from the fish sauce, and a sugary sweetness to boot. A little something for every place on your tongue.

Juice of 1 lime

1 tablespoon fish sauce

1 tablespoon sugar

1 tablespoon water

Pinch of red pepper flakes

★

Hoisin Drizzle

Hoisin, which means "sea-faring sauce" in Chinese, is a jam-like condiment made from wheat or soybeans whose flavors typically include garlic and chilies. A sealed jar lasts next to forever in the fridge. In this dipping sauce, its salty, fruity qualities sauce team with the lemony tartness and the subtle nuttiness of the sesame oil.

2 tablespoons hoisin sauce

Juice of ½ lemon

1 teaspoon sesame oil

¼ teaspoon sugar

★

Honeyed Orange Dipping Sauce

Here again a balancing act: sweetness from the honey, acidity from the orange juice, and saltiness from the fish and soy sauces. What it lacks in modesty, it makes up for with exuberance.

¼ cup orange juice

2 tablespoons light soy sauce

2 tablespoons honey

¼ teaspoon fish sauce

4 slices of bread, crusts removed (cinnamon-raisin, buttercrust, whole wheat, brown or other soft-textured breads)

2 tablespoons unsalted butter, melted

Your choice of filling (see ideas on page 137)

A sprinkling of sugar

★

MAKES 4 TURNOVERS

Here's how to turn a lowly slice of soft sandwich bread into a lowly turnover. You'll be surprised at what a little brushing of butter can do. These quickly executed turnovers are ideal for overtired kids, as well as overworked parents.

While we've offered up a range of fillings to tuck or spread inside, you should improvise to your heart's content.

★ ★ ★

★ Preheat the oven to 400°F.

★ Roll out the crust-free bread with a rolling pin. The bread should be flattened to the thickness of a saltine.

★ Brush the edges of the bread with the melted butter. In the center of each, spoon a generous tablespoon of filling; for spreadable items such as peanut butter or applesauce, cover all but the edges of the bread.

★ Fold the bread into a triangle and press the edges together. Crimp the seam with a fork if necessary. Set the turnovers on a baking sheet.

★ Brush the top of each turnover with additional butter and sprinkle with sugar. Bake until golden brown, about 20 minutes.

FULFILLING FILLINGS

★ A spoonful of preserves and a smear of cream cheese

★ A dollop of jelly and a layer of peanut butter

★ Semisweet chocolate bits or bars (to fashion a mock pain au chocolat)

★ Brie, applesauce, and chopped walnuts

★ A smear of goat cheese with pumpkin or apple butter

★ Fresh berries (or peach or plum slices) with a sprinkling of sugar

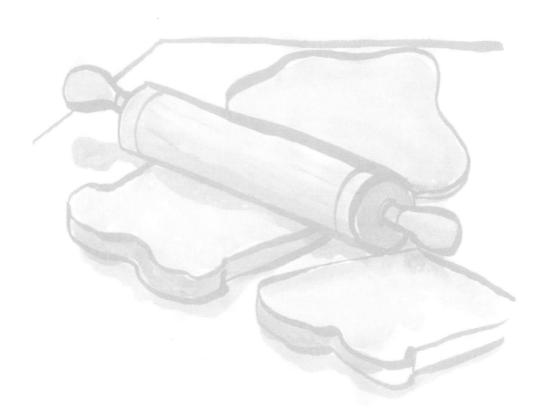

Toastwiches

We have all had that sudden hunger pang, stared at the paltry offerings inside the fridge, and ended up slathering bologna with mayo or squirting mustard on cold grilled bratwursts and going to bed, only to wake an hour later, desperately searching for Tums.

For this hour's menu we searched for midnight melts that won't lead to nightmarish meltdowns. We tested Australian jaffles, Italian panini, the French *croque monsieur*. We found, but hesitated to try, dozens of thrifty wartime "toastwiches" from sixty years ago, when "stretching" ingredients such as beef was considered part of the stateside war effort.

Recipes—or, by definition, a lack of recipes—surround the "Dagwood Bumstead," the classic comic strip's improvised colossus of bread, meats, and cheeses. You hardly need us to suggest a combination; we'd only discourage you from undertaking anything taller than your fist after the witching hour. (Attention Alfred Portale fans: Presenting obelisks and pyramids of food should be confined to daytime hours.)

And few of us would rise to the occasion and vie for the sandwich-making world record at this hour. Last year, folks in Nizhni Novgorod tried for a place in the *Guinness Book of World Records* by building "Russia's largest sandwich" in three hours. It measured 16.97 meters and contained 100 kilograms of mayonnaise and 100 kilograms of bread. The sandwich fed 2,000 people. (Do linger a moment on that mayo/bread ratio. And remember, in some parts of the former empire, the buttering of cheese is standard fare.)

Here, instead, are toasts that don't require a bottle of bubbly or a crowd of friends clinking glasses. These are toasts you offer yourself: toasts with figs, toasts with cheeses, toasts with mashed tomatoes, toasts-turned-tarts, and even a toast of sorts created from day-old doughnuts. So here's a toast to pumpernickel, sourdough, buttercrust, whole wheat, and all the good-night goodness those grains can bring.

the good-night goodness of grains

Smooshed Tomato Toasts

One ½-inch-thick slice
of peasant bread

1 clove garlic, peeled

1 ripe tomato, halved
at its equator

Extra virgin olive oil

Salt and freshly
ground pepper

Coarsely grated Parmigiano-
Reggiano cheese, optional

★

SERVES 1

This is a summertime staple to use when tomatoes cry out to be eaten morning, noon, and night. Seek out heirloom tomatoes when you can, if only for the pleasure of imagining your great-grandfather growing these very plants. Just calling the roll of the many varieties is an undeniable pleasure: Mr. Stripey, Brandywine, Persimmon, Box Car Willy, Zogola, Stump o' the World, Boondock, Amana Orange, Stakebreaker, San Francisco Fog, Earl of Edgecombe, Aunt Ginny's Purple, Jaune Coeur de Pigeon—hey, why not try counting heirloom tomatoes instead of sheep?

★ ★ ★

★ Toast the bread and then, while it is still hot, rub with the garlic clove.

★ Smoosh (there's no other word for it) the tomato into the garlic-rubbed side of the toast.

★ Sprinkle the tomato with olive oil, salt and pepper, and the cheese if you can't resist.

Plowman's Toast

Not to be confused with French toast, this is an appealing plowman's lunch: a single course of fruit, bread, and cheese, all toasted together for a few charming bites. You can fashion a slice of this any time you're tempted to feign a British accent and confess that you're feeling a tad peckish. (Just don't expect the butler to fetch it for you.)

★ ★ ★

★ Preheat the oven to 400°F or use a toaster oven.

★ Toast the bread. Be ever so English: do remove the crusts.

★ Arrange the leaves on the toast and layer with the slices of pear and peels of cheese (use a vegetable peeler on the cold cheese). Sprinkle with freshly ground pepper.

★ Pop into the oven for several minutes, or until the cheese has begun to melt.

★ Serve warm.

VARIATION

When there's a bounty of fresh tomatoes (pronounced toe-MAH-toes), replace the pear with a thick slice.

---

1 thick slice of peasant or sourdough bread

A few leaves of spinach, watercress, or arugula

1 small ripe pear, peeled, cored, and sliced

3 ounces Stilton or a sharp cheddar

Freshly ground pepper

★

SERVES 1

2 ripe nectarines or peaches,
cut into slices

4 slices of sourdough bread,
½ to ¾ inch thick

2 tablespoons unsalted
butter, softened

2 tablespoons peach or
apricot preserves or
orange marmalade

Freshly grated nutmeg

¼ cup packed brown sugar

Sour cream, vanilla yogurt,
or crème fraîche

★

SERVES 4

Here's another extemporaneous way to bake up a personal tartlet for bedtime. It's hardly more trouble than whipping up a couple slices of cinnamon toast, and it delivers the extra lusciousness of warmed fruit. What's more, the basic premise can be expanded into a family-size dessert. Just promise faithfully that you'll actually save some for the family.

★ ★ ★

★ Preheat the broiler or toaster oven.

★ Halve and pit the fruit.

★ Toast the sliced bread until it turns light brown. Butter each piece and spread it with jam. Top the toasts with slices of fruit and sprinkle with nutmeg and brown sugar.

★ Arrange the fruit toasts on a small baking sheet and place under the broiler (or place on the tray in the toaster oven). Broil the toasts until the sugar has caramelized and the fruit is warm, about 5 minutes.

★ Serve with a dollop of sour cream, vanilla yogurt, or crème fraîche.

VARIATIONS

Spiced mascarpone cheese and plums: Mix 1 cup of mascarpone with a pinch of garam masala (a fragrant Indian spice combination) or pumpkin pie seasoning. Spread this on the toasted bread and top with sliced plums. Broil as instructed above.

Huntsman cheese and apples: Wash, core, and cut 2 apples into 8 pieces each. Crumble a small chunk of huntsman cheese and dab it on the toasted bread. Arrange 4 apple wedges on top of the cheese and broil the toasts.

NOTE: To improvise the tang and bite of hunstman cheese, use equal parts blue cheese and mild cheddar.

Double-down Doughnuts

Doughnuts are like manna from heaven—a bit heavier, perhaps. True, we don't know anyone who can eat doughnuts with impunity. (But we also don't know anyone who wouldn't love to have retained the imperviousness of a high-school student's stomach.)

In this defiant indulgence, grilling caramelizes the sugar glaze, flattening the little cakes and yet elevating them . . . bringing them down to earth like manna.

Our first choice is cinnamon cake doughnuts, the staple of every bakery or doughnut shop. Glazed or powdered sugar doughnuts also become ethereal with this grilling. It's the goo-filled you must resist.

★ ★ ★

★ Melt the butter in a grill pan or a skillet over low heat for 2 minutes. Arrange the doughnut slices, cut side up, in the pan. Cover with a heavy plate to weigh them down. Cook until the doughnut halves are golden and the sugar has caramelized.

★ Flip them over and give the cake side a brief turn—just a minute or so to tan.

★ Enjoy this irresistible treat with warmed applesauce or apple butter, or dunk the slices in cold apple cider or dark black coffee.

1 tablespoon butter

1 day-old cinnamon cake doughnut, halved (like a bagel)

Applesauce or apple butter, optional

★

SERVES 1

Figgy Toasts

2 slices sourdough bread

2 teaspoons olive oil

**2 tablespoons
mascarpone cheese**

2 fresh figs, sliced

**1 tablespoon crumbled
blue cheese**

A few walnuts, chopped

**Drizzle of balsamic vinegar
or black fig vinegar**

★

SERVES 2

These oiled, crisped, slathered, cheesed, and sprinkled toasts may be the headiest morsel in our late-night repertoire. Many dishes are imaginable; you read the ingredients and conjure up the taste sensation in your mind. But this crusty bite is unimaginably delicious; your nose and taste buds must sample it in order to compound the different textures and flavors.

And now a word about fresh figs. In this recipe, dried ones won't do. We have substituted plums with some impunity, although friends devoted to the original recipe never fail to mention how they miss the figs. What can we say? Not only are figs unmistakably figs, but they are little punching bags of nutrition, providing vitamins A, B, C, folic acid, calcium, copper, iron, manganese, potassium, and zinc—not that you'll be sensing anything but their resinous sweetness amid the cheese and vinegar's aromatic creaminess.

★ Toast the bread and then drizzle each slice with olive oil.

★ Smear the toasts with mascarpone cheese.

★ Place the figs on top of the cheese and sprinkle with flecks of blue cheese and walnuts. Dot with a few drops of vinegar.

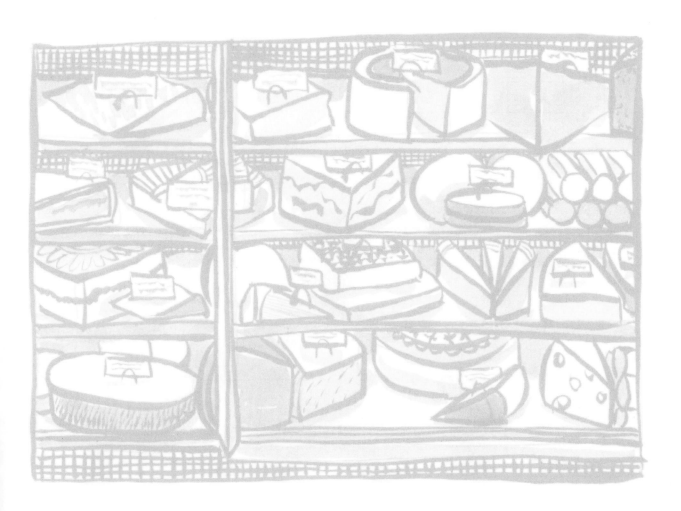

Skinny Dips & Other Rarebits

HoW can you still be hungry? You had dinner, right? And then at 10:15 you cooked up the mashed-potato pancakes. At 11:45 you dipped a few macaroons in chocolate. Delicious. You baked the Parmesan wafers at 12:15. Fine. So now, an hour later, your stomach's still grumbling?

It's understandable. Perhaps you're wearing a cast or your back is aching and you just can't get comfortable. Maybe you're lying awake because you're due to deliver any day now, or maybe it's your daughter who's in labor and you're waiting for the call announcing your new grandchild. Maybe you've just rung off the phone after two hours of amateur psychology counseling with a friend (on the West Coast, where it's still early, thank you very much!).

Or perhaps you're having a bout of insomnia. Why? Why now? The only thing more mysterious than its causes is its possible cures . . . and we've heard them all. We've even tried a few ourselves: chamomile tea, alarm clocks with the soothing sounds of nature-turned-monotony, magnetic mattresses that mystically improve circulation, and so forth. It was the "so forth" that kept us awake: listening to the white noise of cheap fans; smelling sandalwood spritzed on the pillowcases; visualizing clouds drifting slowly, inexorably, endlessly across the ceiling; and even soaking in a hot milk bath (cornstarch and powdered milk), which ended up being a reason to stay up *later* cleaning the tub.

To the rescue, then! Here are five rare and not-so-rarebits you can do up in no time flat. Considering you're only looking for something distracting at this point, there's nothing too heavy or formidable. Just dunk the suggested fruits, breads, or vegetables and imagine each morsel is one of your niggling worries sliding into oblivion down your throat. Skinny-dip your way to a carefree sleep.

the soothing sounds of nature-turned-monotony

Fondue for One

2 tablespoons unsalted butter

1 large shallot, finely chopped

1 small clove garlic, minced

½ cup chicken broth or white wine (or a combination)

1 tablespoon all-purpose flour

¼ pound high-quality blue cheese

1 teaspoon Dijon mustard

Pinch of salt

Pinch of freshly ground pepper

½ cup chopped toasted walnuts, optional

★

MAKES 1¼ CUPS

You may be fond of fondue—and we've found that everyone is—but making it probably means you have to drag out the kitchen stool to reach into the little cabinet over the refrigerator and retrieve the twice-used fondue pot your mother gave you at her last garage sale. You might also be a bit reluctant to cook up a vat of melted cheese for your lone self. This recipe captures the essence of the fondue experience without requiring the usual equipment, though we know you'll miss having the little tin of Sterno waving its wan blue flame under the big pot.

Serve this cheesy pool with bread crusts (try pumpernickel, rye, or sourdough), sliced pears and apples, red and yellow bell pepper slices, or other vegetables. The recipe makes enough for you to dip to your heart's content and still have some left to share or to reheat later in the week, when the fondue won't have lost any of its charm.

★ In a microwave-safe bowl, combine the butter, shallot, and garlic. Cover the bowl with plastic wrap and zap the mixture on high for 3 minutes.

★ Add the chicken broth. Microwave uncovered for 3 more minutes.

★ Add the flour and microwave again for 1 minute. Stir, then add the crumbled blue cheese, mustard, salt, and pepper. Microwave once more for 1 or 2 minutes.

★ Once the fondue is smooth, stir in the nuts . . . and go nuts.

Welsh Not-so-Rarebit

"Rarebit" or "rabbit"? The question has plagued us ever since we first saw Mother pour a puddle of orange cheese from a convenient boil-in-the-bag pouch. Dictionaries are no help. Under "rarebit" they say, "see 'rabbit.'" And then when you "see" rabbit, the last definition (after mentioning our floppy-eared friend, TV antenna, and chopping someone on the back of the neck—"rabbit punch") reads, "Welsh rabbit, a dish of melted or toasted cheese on toast." Call this dish whatever you like; it has a much richer heritage than 1960s convenience food.

- ★ Melt the butter in a saucepan over medium heat.
- ★ Whisk in the flour and cook for 2 or 3 minutes; the flour should turn a caramel color. Add the nutmeg, mustard, cayenne, black pepper, and the saffron, if desired.
- ★ Whisk in the milk and cook the mixture until it thickens, 2 or 3 additional minutes. The sauce should coat the back of a wooden spoon.
- ★ Lower the heat and add the grated cheese a little at a time, allowing each addition to melt before adding more.
- ★ Check the seasoning carefully. If salt is necessary, add it now. (Since the various cheeses traditionally used in this dish have varying degrees of saltiness—even within the same variety—the salt should be withheld until this chance to sample the completed dish.)
- ★ Serve warm over toast, or pour over noodles or grilled tomatoes.

2 tablespoons unsalted butter

3 tablespoons all-purpose flour

Grating of nutmeg

Pinch of dry mustard

Pinch of cayenne pepper

Freshly ground pepper

Pinch of saffron threads, optional

1 cup whole milk or beer

2 cups grated cheese, such as Gruyère, English farmhouse cheddar, or mild Swiss (or a combination)

Salt

Toast, noodles, or grilled tomatoes for serving

★

SERVES 2 GENEROUSLY

All Dal-ed Up

½ cup dried red lentils

1 cup water

2 tablespoons vegetable oil

1 tablespoon grated fresh ginger

1 small clove garlic, minced

½ cup chopped onion

½ teaspoon ground cumin

1 teaspoon garam masala

1 teaspoon curry powder

½ cup coconut cream (see Note below)

Juice of 1 lemon

Salt and freshly ground pepper

6 cilantro sprigs, coarsely chopped

¼ cup almond slices, toasted

★

MAKES 1½ CUPS

Dal, *or* dhal, *is the Indian word for a dish of cooked pulses.* Pulses *is a word that means the dried seeds of any number of legumes, including lentils, mung beans, and peas. Take our word for it—this makes an unusual, creamy, and appetizing dip for vegetables or a spread that expands the possibilities for vegetarian sandwiches. Since the lentils are rather earth-toned (as in drab), if you're serving this to others you might want to doll up the dal with slivered almonds, thin lemon wheels, or pitted olive halves.*

★ ★ ★

★ Place the lentils in a large microwave-safe bowl. Add the water, cover with plastic wrap, and microwave for 10 minutes. You should have about 1 cup of lentils. Empty them into a serving dish and set aside.

★ Combine the oil, ginger, garlic, and onion in the bowl. Cover and microwave for 2 minutes.

★ Add the cumin, garam masala, curry powder, coconut cream, lemon juice, salt, and pepper. Microwave for an additional 2 minutes.

★ Return the cooked lentils to the bowl, stir to combine everything, and microwave the lentils for 4 more minutes. Stir once more halfway through the heating.

★ Add the chopped cilantro, spoon the mixture into the serving bowl, and sprinkle with the toasted almonds. Serve warm.

NOTE: Coconut cream comes from the first pressing of the coconut. It's equivalent to the first cold pressing of extra virgin olive oil. It is somewhat thick and has a gray cast. It needs to be tempered, or it can curdle. Coconut milk is the second extraction. It has a thinner consistency. A third product, sweetened coconut milk, is typically used in piña coladas and should not be used in land-locked areas, much less in this recipe.

Nutty Tofu Spread

At 190 calories per 2 tablespoons, perhaps peanut butter isn't the ideal thing to be scarfing down before bed, when your body is more likely to be storing than burning fat. So here's a way to lighten up peanut butter to use not only as a spread for bread, but also as a dip for vegetables or a schmear in a lettuce- or rice-paper wrap. If you want it sweeter, omit the garlic and Tabasco.

★ ★ ★

★ Blend all the ingredients—that's about it. A food processor, submersible mixer, or hand mixer will do nicely.

½ cup peanut butter
(natural style, without
hydrogenated oil)

⅓ cup firm tofu

3 tablespoons brown sugar

2 tablespoons lime juice

2 tablespoons low-sodium
soy sauce

A few drops of Tabasco
sauce, or pinch of
cayenne pepper

2 cloves garlic, crushed

★

MAKES 1 CUP

¾ cup extra virgin olive oil

¼ cup balsamic vinegar

1 tablespoon maple syrup

3 cloves garlic, crushed

½ teaspoon grated
lemon zest

Pinch of crushed
red pepper flakes

1 teaspoon chopped
fresh thyme or ¼ teaspoon
dried thyme

1 teaspoon chopped
fresh rosemary or
¼ teaspoon dried rosemary

1 teaspoon chopped
fresh basil or ¼ teaspoon
dried basil

1 tablespoon chopped
flat-leaf parsley

2 tablespoons grated
Parmesan cheese

½ teaspoon freshly
ground pepper

★

MAKES 1 CUP

You'll find many uses for this exceptionally versatile dressing—you're bound to, since it will keep for two weeks in the refrigerator. It wields a potent garlic punch and eventually accumulates a bit of heat, but the sweetness of the maple syrup and the balsamic vinegar balance the assertiveness. Because a little of the dressing offers so much flavor, it's an excellent choice for dunking veggies or bread bits—also known as skinny-dipping after dark.

★ ★ ★

★ Mix all the ingredients together and drizzle over a piece of toast. Or dip spears of Belgian endive and celery into the mix.

★ For serving, use toast or spears of Belgian endives or celery sticks.

Cucumber Slurry

Officially known as terituan, *a Persian dip often served at supper with lettuce leaves, this cool, blended slurry makes an easy transition into late-night snacking. The trick is to consume it the instant it's concocted in order to savor the confluence of the walnuts' crunch, the herbs' leafy bite, the garlic's slight heat, and the cucumber's faint fragrance. Less cool than the usual cucumber, this salsa is the color of sea foam. Dunk into it with flax-seed bread, romaine lettuce leaves, or other raw or cooked vegetables. Or add a healthy splash of vodka and give that cuke something to crow about.*

★ ★ ★

★ Chop half of the cucumber. Cut the other half into thick wedges for dipping later.

★ In the bowl of a food processor or blender, combine the chopped cucumber and the garlic, walnuts, sea salt, basil, mint, parsley, vinegar, and olive oil. Blend until minced rather than puréed.

1 cucumber, peeled and seeded

1 small clove garlic, minced

¼ cup walnuts, finely chopped

1 teaspoon sea salt

1 teaspoon chopped fresh basil or a pinch of dried basil

1 teaspoon chopped fresh mint or a pinch of dried mint

1 tablespoon chopped flat-leaf parsley

2 teaspoons red wine vinegar

¼ cup extra virgin olive oil

★

MAKES 1 CUP

2 teaspoons olive oil

**2 shallots, peeled and
chopped**

**10 shiitake mushrooms,
cleaned and coarsely chopped**

4 ounces firm tofu

1 tablespoon tamari

Dash of favorite hot sauce

**Salt and freshly ground
pepper**

**1 teaspoon flax seeds or
sesame seeds**

★

MAKES 1 CUP

The shiitake mushroom is a contender for nature's most healthy offering. Just check out its credentials: it boasts all eight essential amino acids in better proportions than most meats and grains; it produces a fat-absorbing compound that aids in weight reduction; it lowers cholesterol and blood pressure; and it possesses antifungal (clearly, it takes one to know one) and cancer-fighting powers. All this, plus having a heady, earthy taste that puts to shame the wan button mushrooms that monopolize the grocers' shelves.

Not only is this paté a delectable dip for vegetables or rice crackers, but also a tablespoon or two adds a flavorful enrichment in a last-minute stew or soup.

Dried Shiitake Mushrooms

If fresh mushrooms are not available, dried shiitakes can stand in. Reconstitute them by soaking the same number of dried mushrooms in the least amount of boiling water that will cover them. In 10 or 15 minutes, the shiitakes should be ready for chopping. Incorporate them into the recipe above and save the strained liquid for another use, such as soup stock. Dried shiitakes often come in large bags; since they store indefinitely, they are a great item to keep tightly sealed in your pantry.

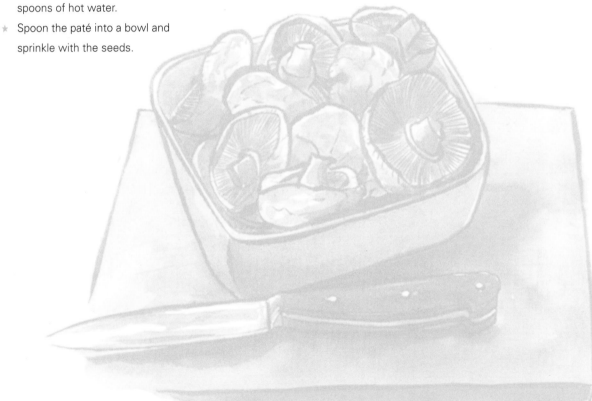

★ ★ ★

- ★ In a microwave-safe bowl, combine the olive oil and shallots. Cover with plastic wrap and microwave for 2 minutes.
- ★ Add the mushrooms and microwave for an additional 2 minutes.
- ★ Add the tofu and tamari. Smash the tofu into the warm mixture. Add the hot sauce, salt, and pepper. For a thinner consistency, mix in a few table-spoons of hot water.
- ★ Spoon the paté into a bowl and sprinkle with the seeds.

2:00 AM

LoVe

TriaNgles

What else is there to eat at two in the morning, when you're ravenous from amorous calorie expenditure, but the most sensuous foods? Foods of love. And just what are these? Oysters have been universally touted, but few of us are inclined to maintain a raw bar at home. Everyone from Ovid to Erzulie (the Haitian sex goddess) has extolled the lust-provoking powers of basil. Others praise lobster. Some asparagus. Many favor chocolate.

We ransacked the annals of the world's cuisines, the myriad cultures of humankind, the pages of *Cosmopolitan* magazine, and we were astonished at the range of foods reputed to increase fertility or sexiness or drive. Here's what we found: If a food is hot, warm, soft, juicy, tangy, sweet, salty, moist, sinewy, or slippery . . . if it's smoky, dense, dark, gingery, airy, earthy, aromatic, spicy, piquant, potent, or tart . . . if it possesses a bite, ignites a peppery glow, burns a little on the lips, beckons the teeth to bite or chew or nibble (or anything that doesn't bring up the topic of flossing) . . . if it has seeds, a husk, a shell, a skin, a peel, or any texture at all . . . if you can slice it, pop it, grind it, drizzle it, nestle it, smooth it, set it aflame, or even stare at it longingly before tossing it down the disposal—it's someone's idea of an aphrodisiac.

Obviously, it's mind over matter. It's probably the "how," not the "what," that makes the food of love. *How* you share it. *How* you think of it. Try this game the next time you're propped up in bed after making love. You name the food and have your partner make it sound sensuous. The object, of course, is to pick a food that could never sound sexy. Shredded wheat? *(Ah, but just holding the brittle pillows on your tongue and sensing the moisture that, slowly, ever so lovely, tempts them to yield . . . etc.)*

And with that, we leave you to linger over aphrodisiacs. Here, instead, are a few *after*-disiacs, something to whip up in the kitchen and bring back to bed, something luscious to cap off a giddy night, something moderately enchanting that won't tax lips that are tender from kissing.

sensuous foods . . . Foods of love

2 tablespoons olive oil

1 flour tortilla

2 tablespoons whipped
cream cheese

2 slices Norwegian
smoked salmon

1 tablespoon snipped fresh
dill or fennel leaves

1 tablespoon roughly
chopped flat-leaf parsley

1 tablespoon capers

1 cup shredded salad greens
(roll up the leaves and slice
into long shreds), optional

1 fried egg, optional

1 squeeze of fresh
lemon juice

Freshly ground pepper

★

MAKES 4 TRIANGLES

This lavish triangle begs for no more than a moment of your time, so you'll be scurrying back to bed before the heat has dissipated from the sheets. Rather than double the tortillas to compose a quesadilla, we take a single round, pan-fry it in a flash, and create a crispy platform for the traditional fixings of lox and bagels: salmon, cream cheese, capers, dill, and—well, we've left off the onions in deference to the occasion.

★ ★ ★

- In a small nonstick skillet, heat 1 tablespoon of the olive oil. When the oil is hot, slide in the flour tortilla. Brown the tortilla, then flip it over.
- Spoon small dollops of the cream cheese over the browned side and spread them with the back of the spoon.
- Delicately place the slices of smoked salmon on top of the cream cheese. The second side of the tortilla should be brown by now.
- Slide the tortilla onto a plate. Drizzle with the remaining tablespoon of olive oil and sprinkle with the dill, parsley, and capers. If you want to create a more substantial dish, add the salad greens and fried egg.
- Squeeze on a bit of lemon juice and season with pepper. Cut the tortilla into four narrow wedges and start triangulating.

1 medium tomato, diced

½ cup seeded and diced
cucumber

½ cup cooked or canned
chickpeas

2 medium red-skin potatoes,
cooked and sliced

2 teaspoons diced canned
green chilies (or less,
depending on your desire
for heat)

1 tablespoon coarsely
chopped fresh cilantro

½ teaspoon garam masala

Dash of Worcestershire sauce

Sea salt and freshly ground
pepper

½ cup puffed rice cereal, such
as Rice Krispies

★

SERVES 2

This offbeat salad, traditionally served in a newspaper cup alongside hot tea, is based on the common fare of street vendors in India, where the cucumber claims its first champions. Indeed, cucumbers have been cultivated there for 3,000 years and eaten for 8,000 more, although the cuke's wild ancestors were hardly burpless and were certainly bitter enough to be low on the list of silk and spice and everything nice the monarchs of Europe demanded of their voyaging explorers.

We have Columbus to thank for the arrival of cucumbers in America. We have physicians of the 1600s to thank for the expression "cool as a cucumber" because of their practice of having fever victims lie on a bed of cucumbers. (The treatment was as effective as lounging in a vat of stewed prunes or sleeping on Parker House rolls.)

We offer you this newspaper cone as another love triangle: something to eat on the balcony after making love. Something for standing in the hallway while you wait for the shower. Or something entirely novel to serve when it's your turn to host the book club.

- Mix the tomato, cucumber, chickpeas, potatoes, chilies, cilantro, garam masala, Worcestershire sauce, sea salt, and pepper in a bowl. Sample a bite, adding salt and pepper to taste.
- Fold a sheet of newspaper to the size of a legal pad. Read whatever it is you want to read, because there's no following the story once you fill the paper with salad.
- Add a piece of waxed paper about the same size and roll the 2 papers to form a small cone. Fold up the point to make a drip-proof bottom. Repeat to make another cone.
- Mix the cereal into the salad and fill the cones. (Adding the cereal at the last moment keeps it crispy. If the salad sits and gets soggy, add more cereal to revive it.)

Wanton Wontons

While fresh wonton wrappers or skins are more frequently deep-fried or steamed, they can also be baked in an instant. Even if they aren't quite as light as phyllo dough or rice paper, they hardly add much weight to the plate. And the good news is fresh wontons are increasingly available at supermarkets, in addition to their usual hangout in Asian groceries.

Here are three crispy wanton ways to use the wontons: a nifty pastry shell, a makeshift toast pocket, and a handy dipping chip.

Wonton Skinnies

¼ cup diced fruit, such as mangoes, or berries

1 tablespoon dark rum

4 small wonton wrappers

1 tablespoon unsalted butter, melted

1 tablespoon sugar

Pinch of Chinese five-spice powder

1 dollop sour cream or crème fraîche

★

MAKES 4 "SKINNIES"

This is exactly like a marvelous mille-feuilles, except it's a deux-feuilles, and it takes about a hundredth of the time required for the French pastry. A brushing of butter elevates the limp little wrappers into a snappy crust—a light pie shell for the fragrant fruit bits.

★ ★ ★

★ Preheat the oven to 400°F.
★ In a small bowl, toss the fruit with the rum and let it macerate a bit.
★ Paint both sides of the wrappers with butter and set them, without overlapping, on a baking sheet. Combine the sugar and five-spice powder and sprinkle the wontons with it.
★ Bake the wrappers for 5 to 7 minutes, until they're golden brown.
★ Place the crisps on plates and top each one with the juicy fruit pieces and a dollop of sour cream or crème fraîche. For a more theatrical staging, you can cut the squares into fourths before baking, to layer the smaller squares with the fruit and cream.

LOVE
TRIANGLES

Wonton Pockets

Here's a more savory way to use these versatile wrappers. The toaster oven makes perfect sense for cooking them.

★ ★ ★

- ★ Preheat the oven to 400°F.
- ★ Place 1 teaspoon of the black bean dip in the center of each wonton wrapper. Dampen the edges of the wrapper with water, fold it in half, and seal the edges.
- ★ Lightly brush both sides of each package with oil and place them on a baking sheet. Bake until golden brown, 5 or 6 minutes.
- ★ Serve warm with the sour cream, guacamole, or salsa, if desired.

VARIATIONS

Instead of the black bean filling, try one of these combinations:

- ★ Sauté a handful of mushrooms with a bit of butter and a teaspoon of chopped scallions
- ★ Mash a bit of cream cheese with some smoked fish or cooked shellfish
- ★ Mix together equal parts feta and cream cheese, adding a pinch of fresh chives

1 tablespoon black bean dip

4 small wonton wrappers

Vegetable oil for brushing

Sour cream, guacamole, or salsa, optional

★

MAKES 4 POCKETS

Making Your Own Crème Fraîche

While most upscale cheesemongers and groceries carry crème fraîche in the dairy section, you can create your own. It will, however, take some time to thicken. Simply combine 1 cup heavy cream and 2 tablespoons cultured buttermilk in a small bowl, cover with plastic wrap and a towel, and set in a warm place for 12 to 24 hours, until the mixture thickens. Store the crème fraîche in the fridge, where it will stay fresh for a week.

Zesty Wonton Triangles

Baked and spiced, these wrappers are like thin and zesty tortillas—they hardly need an accompanying dip. The egg-white wash can adhere any number of seasonings, so experiment with some of your favorites: caraway, cumin, or fennel seeds; a sprinkling of dried mixed herbs; sesame seeds and sea salt; curry powder.

★ ★ ★

5 wonton wrappers, each cut on the diagonal to form 2 triangles

1 egg white, lightly beaten with a fork or whisk

½ teaspoon chili powder

½ teaspoon ground cumin

½ teaspoon salt

½ teaspoon freshly ground pepper

★

MAKES 10 TRIANGLES

★ Preheat the oven to 350°F. Coat a baking sheet with cooking spray.

★ Place the wonton triangles on the baking sheet. Brush each with the beaten egg white.

★ Combine the spices and sprinkle the mixture over the wontons. Bake until golden brown, about 5 minutes. Let cool. Let crunch.

Flambé the Night Away

Here's a way to light up the night that's a bit more sophisticated than a plug-in plastic shell covering a tiny bulb. You don't need to have earned a fire-safety merit badge to undertake this dessert, but you do need to pay attention when you set fire to the pan of sautéing fruit. It's too late to try impressing your date with your pyrotechnics—unless you're between the sheets.

★ ★ ★

★ In a chafing dish or nonstick skillet, melt the butter and add the sugar, stirring until it dissolves.

★ Add the fruit and heat thoroughly for 3 to 5 minutes.

★ In a separate small pan (or in a glass measuring cup placed in the microwave), warm the brandy; it should feel hot to the touch but nowhere near simmering.

★ Pour the brandy over the cooking fruit and, taking care to execute this next move quickly, touch an edge of the brandy's surface with a lit match.

★ Shake the pan, stir carefully, and tame those flames. Set a scoop of ice cream atop each slice of cake and pour the fruit and extinguished sauce on top.

2 tablespoons unsalted butter

2 tablespoons dark
brown sugar

2 bananas, peeled and split;
2 mangoes, peeled and pitted;
2 nectarines or peaches,
pitted and cut into quarters;
1 cup sour cherries, pitted;
or 5 figs, cut in half

2 to 3 ounces brandy,
framboise, Grand Marnier,
dark rum, or other liqueur

2 scoops vanilla ice cream
or frozen yogurt

2 slices pound cake or
angel food cake

★

SERVES 2

2:30 AM

Late-Night
Rehab

We've always been amused by hangover cures. Hitting the sack after several rounds of margaritas can be challenging. All right, "challenging" doesn't cover it. And that's why hundreds of likely, unlikely, and downright loathsome concoctions are touted.

Our interest was piqued recently by a British company that plans to market Soba, a powdered green volcanic rock that purports to be an "alcohol magnet," attracting the alcohol and expelling it from your system like an internal bouncer. Meanwhile, a Russian firm is launching a pickled hangover cure based on a popular rejuvenator: drinking the juice of salted cucumbers. Beet and cabbage flavors are also in development.

In search of other time-tested remedies, we consulted the voices of experience: college students. Cat, a coed from Seattle, writes, "Start your night of drinking with a dose of vitamin B_{12} and a big glass of water. Drink 2 glasses of water and take another B_{12} before bed. In the morning, down another B_{12} with 2 more glasses of water."

Jonnie at UCLA offers this suggestion: "Sleep until 11:00 A.M., then run out to a fast-food place for a cheeseburger, fries, and chocolate shake. Chase it with a can of Coke." It's a caffeine/sugar/fat buzz that stokes the internal engine.

Melissa in Pittsburgh suggests the best remedy is not drinking in the first place. Shall we move on?

Bob from Canton submitted this tonic: "Put 8 ounces of tomato juice, a banana, 4 ice cubes, and 2 aspirins into a blender. Blend. Drink in one continuous gulp."

Joan from Atlanta states: "The only cure is fried liver." But Joan is mistaken. There are as many ways of undoing as there are ways of overdoing. We've chosen three restorative recipes that are satisfying enough to eat even when you're sober.

And because people find themselves awake at this hour for other reasons—insomniacs or night owls with a legitimate excuse to eschew the bed—we also offer four energy-boosting drinks. As for the insomniacs, there's no better prescription than W. C. Fields's sage advice: "The best cure for insomnia is to get a lot of sleep."

Four Energizers

Finishing the last of the Christmas cards . . . packing your daughter's luggage for college . . . studying for your oral exams—there are nights when you have to burn the midnight oil and need food, glorious food, to supplement your energy. For those times we offer the following power-packed potions. The protein and ginseng will stimulate the brain. The magnesium and calcium will provide nutrients for muscle and nerve function. Hearing the wailing screech of the blender will also enliven things, as will neglecting to secure the blender lid tightly enough.

For the fatigued brain, you need a shake that's rich in protein as well as carbohydrates. On the other hand, smoothies that are high in sugar and complex carbohydrates will increase serotonin production and put you to sleep in a hurry.

If you find yourself inclined toward smoothies on a regular basis, enhance their nutritional content by stocking a few supplements, such as the brewer's yeast, ginseng, and protein powder mentioned below. These small additions contribute a large number of nutrients; no, you may not substitute Snickers bars.

★ ★ ★

★ To whip up any of these drinks, for one, combine all the ingredients in a blender jar and purée until smooth. Gulp the concoction straight from the jar, or find a big glass and a sippy straw and take the drink back to work.

Ginseng-Sling

A large branching taproot that resembles ginger root, ginseng contains chemicals clev-erly termed ginsenosides, *which are thought to counter physical fatigue and enhance mental awareness by balancing the hypothyroid-pituitary-adrenal axis—you know, that thing that makes us sit up straight and act like ladies and gentlemen.*

As for brewer's yeast, it offers up B vitamins and chromium, which regulate blood sugar levels, keeping you from carbohydrate shocks and sugar crashes.

The rest of the ingredients are for decoration.

NOTE: Of course, we don't expect every household to stock ginseng tablets. But if you are the night-owl type, anticipate such a nighttime need and purchase a small bottle at the local pharmacy or health food store. Ginseng also comes in liquid and powder forms.

1 cup milk or soy milk

1 frozen banana, chunked, or 8 to 10 frozen strawberries

1 small scoop protein powder

1 teaspoon brewer's yeast

1 ginseng tablet (see Note) dissolved in 1 tablespoon hot water

1 teaspoon vanilla extract

Mocha-Java Jolt

Not only does this drink offer the familiar pairing of coffee and chocolate; it also harmo-nizes carbohydrates with proteins (from the milk, yogurt, and powdered supplement), thereby preventing the low blood sugar that invites fatigue. Or maybe it's just the rous-ing double dose of caffeine.

NOTE: If you have refrigerated yogurt rather than frozen yogurt, add that with a few ice cubes to the blender.

1 cup skim milk or soy milk

1 cup vanilla or coffee frozen nonfat yogurt (see Note)

2 tablespoons instant coffee powder

1 scoop protein powder

2 tablespoons chocolate sauce or instant hot chocolate

1 teaspoon vanilla extract

Chocolate Cherry Jubilee

1 cup plain or chocolate
soy milk

1 cup pitted frozen cherries

2 tablespoons unsweetened
cocoa powder

2 tablespoons protein powder

1 tablespoon flax-seed oil

Ice cubes

The indiscernible ingredient in this beverage is flax-seed oil, which contains essential fatty acids. Essentially, it's nothing you're going to focus on at 2:30 in the morning, but the oil works its wonders by tuning your hormonal system even as it temps as an anti-inflammatory. We've called this shake a "jubilee" in hopes of lessening your trepidation regarding flax-seed oil. It merely wants to be your friend.

Cocoa-Nutter Butter

1 cup plain or chocolate
soy milk

1 frozen banana, chunked

2 tablespoons unsweetened
cocoa

2 tablespoons nut butter
(peanut, almond, or cashew)

Ice cubes

Nut butters are high in proteins and fats, which slow the release of glucose into the bloodstream. What's that mean for night owls? This drink will help you feel sated while offsetting the chance of a sugar rush and the achy exhaustion that comes with it.

Nuts also contain folic acid, magnesium, and potassium, which help maintain your concentration and stamina. Add the stimulating effect of cocoa, and you've raised your flagging spirits up the up-all-night pole.

Punkin Punch

Pumpkin purée, which is not pumpkin-pie filling, creates a nutritious, fiber-rich, and creamy base for a thick orange smoothie drink that's rich in alpha- and beta-carotene—and you know what those are good for, right? Making things orange!

While nothing's better than fresh pumpkin, you can freeze some of the fleshy pulp you cooked during the Halloween carving spree (smaller pumpkins provide tastier pulp) to use in these moments when you need a little antioxidizing.

★ ★ ★

★ Combine all the ingredients except the skim milk in a blender and mix until frothy. Add the skim milk for a thinner shake, if needed.

NOTE: If you'd rather use refrigerated yogurt, you can substitute cup for cup, although you might want to adjust the sweetness depending on the yogurt's sugar content.

½ cup pumpkin purée

Pinch of ground cinnamon

Pinch of ginger

Pinch of ground cloves

1 tablespoon maple syrup or blackstrap molasses

1 cup vanilla frozen nonfat yogurt (see Note below)

Skim milk, as needed

★

SERVES 1

Papaya Pick-Me-Up-and-Put-Me-Down

1 small papaya, peeled,
seeded, and cut into chunks

½ cup freshly squeezed
orange juice

½ cup apple juice

½ medium cucumber,
peeled and seeded

Ice cubes

★

SERVES 1

Try this fortifying concoction to hydrate your system, flush out some lingering impurities, and get your body rebounding with a vitamin booster shot. This drink works best if you remembered to ask your designated driver to find you a papaya on the way home.

★ ★ ★

★ Cast all the ingredients, along with any of the evening's regrets, into the blender and purée.

Why a Papaya?

Papayas arrive at the local market in both the ripened and the unripened stage. For this recipe, you'll want the softer, sweeter, ripened fruit; the papaya should yield slightly when you squeeze it.

Just curious: Since papayas are employed full-time by the folks at Accent (the fruit contains papain, an enzyme that breaks down protein), could the papaya's role as a hangover cure have anything to do with its meat-tenderizing talents?

Quick Greasy-Spooner grits

Ground hominy is among the most basic foodstuffs, and among its manifestations are cheese grits, lovingly hand-stirred by cooks all across the old Confederacy, but also lobbed into bowls at most after-the-bars-close greasy spoons. These grits stick to your ribs for hours and hours, stoking your dying engine with plentiful carbs and fats. Do not, under any circumstances, let your purist southern friends see this blasphemous recipe, since our version suggests you cook this in the microwave. (We just don't think you can be trusted at the stove if you are three sheets to the wind.)

★ Pour the water into a shallow microwave-safe dish. Microwave for 3 minutes or until it boils.

★ Gradually whisk in the grits and salt. Microwave for an additional 3 minutes, or until the mixture has thickened.

★ Stir in the Worcestershire sauce and hot sauce, if using, the cheese mixture, and 1 tablespoon of the butter. Mix until smooth.

★ Crack the eggs on top of the cooked grits and dot with the remaining tablespoon of butter. Sprinkle the eggs and grits with the pepper, cover the dish with plastic wrap, and return it to the microwave for 2 more minutes, or until the eggs are cooked to your liking. Toss on a little extra cheese before serving.

1 cup water

½ cup quick-cooking grits

Pinch of salt

½ teaspoon Worcestershire sauce

Dash of favorite hot sauce, optional

½ cup shredded cheese mixture (Parmesan, cheddar, Swiss), plus additional cheese for topping

2 tablespoons unsalted butter

2 large eggs

Freshly ground pepper

★

SERVES 1 HUNGRY JACK

Son-in-Law's Eggs

This classic hangover remedy, Thai in origin, has a stalwart international following. It works equally well for daughters-in-law and most other relations. The recipe is a bit complicated, so designate someone to be the hangover chef in hopes that they'll be able to follow the directions on your behalf.

★ ★ ★

2 tablespoons plus ¼ cup vegetable oil

2 teaspoons crushed red pepper flakes

3 shallots, minced

2 hard-boiled eggs, peeled

¼ cup maple syrup or palm sugar

¼ cup tamarind juice or Worcestershire sauce (see note)

2 tablespoons fish sauce (a salty condiment found at Asian markets and larger groceries)

2 fresh cilantro sprigs, for garnish

1 chopped scallion, for garnish

★

SERVES 1

★ In a skillet, heat 2 tablespoons of the oil until it begins to smoke. Add the red pepper flakes. Remove the pan from the heat and shake it. Keep your face away from the fumes and don't let the pepper flakes burn.

★ Add the minced shallots and allow them to cook over medium-high heat, until translucent (about 2 minutes). Remove them from the pan, set them aside, and wipe the pan clean with a paper towel.

★ Add the remaining ¼ cup of oil to the pan. Turn the heat to medium; when the oil is hot, add the whole cooked eggs. Brown the eggs on all sides—about 5 minutes total—remove them, and set on a paper towel to blot.

★ Remove all but 2 teaspoons of oil from the pan. Add the maple syrup, tamarind juice, and fish sauce. Cook until you have a thick sauce.

★ Cut the eggs lengthwise and place them, yolk side up, on a plate. Top with the shallots and drizzle with sauce. Garnish with cilantro and chopped scallion.

★ Serve with a chilly beer and an aspirin.

First-shift Foods

You're groggy. You're cranky. You have nothing to say to the world until the coffee wonder machine makes good on its promise and delivers the brewed cup according to the timer you always remember to set.

Or maybe this is *your* hour, when not even the sun is up to distract you from your thoughts, thoughts such as "Why am I not asleep?" You'll write in your journal, copy out the recipe for the peach cake you took to parents' night and the school secretary wanted, paper-clip the coupons into "frozen" and "cleaning" and other useful categories so you can throw them away in groups rather than individually, since they'll never be with you when you're any place you might actually use them—except maybe once, when the ones you need will have expired.

Or maybe you don't need so much sleep? You're going to run six miles, warm up and cool down with stretches, and still be dressed—in a pressed business suit, no less—reviewing the fourth-quarter budget figures as the oatmeal simmers in the pot. No one likes a show-off.

We all need foods to beckon us from bed, to jump-start the brain, to set the gears whirring and the nerves firing and the blood doing that squishy rushing in and out thing the heart makes it do. And most of us would love a staff to serve up the food as well and, while they're at it, set out a pair of matching socks, find the new batteries you bought for the Walkman in your gym bag, highlight just what you need to read in the morning paper, delete the SPAM from your IN box, and empty the cat's litter box—all this before you walk into the kitchen to say, "Good morning."

In the next chapter we'll supply you with fast alternatives to fast food, but here we want you to linger a bit over breakfast, to rise and shine and consider something more than our friend Kent's relentless routine of a frozen bagel brought to life with a thirty-second zap in the microwave and a two-minute suntan in the toaster. We want you to greet the day with something more than our friend Anne's religious commitment to a whole banana that satisfies her sweet tooth and the fistful of vitamins that stands in for the orange juice, bran cereal, soy milk, and low-fat turkey sausages that really would have been nice.

Here are foods that can be a part of your body's wake-up call. Oatmeal, granola, hot cakes, mush: these are reveille rations. Substantive, fortifying, reviving: here is farmhand fodder for when the rooster crows and the early bird gets his worm.

foods to beckon us from bed

Jeweled Gruel

1 bowl hot oatmeal

1 teaspoon unsalted butter

**1 generous handful of
chopped dried fruits
(cranberries, strawberries,
cherries, blueberries,
currants, golden raisins, dark
raisins, apricots, prunes,
peaches, candied orange or
lemon peels, banana chips,
papaya, mangoes . . .)**

**A sprinkle of your favorite
nuts, optional**

**A drizzle of honey or
maple syrup**

★

SERVES 1

If your idea of oatmeal is gruel—a sticky conglomeration made from a packet of powder or a gelled mass burbling on the motel's complementary breakfast bar—we beg you to give oatmeal another look. And not simply because oats provide the soluble fiber that's good for your arteries.

Try thick-cut oats, steel-cut oats, Scottish oatmeal, oatmeal with wheat berries, or even quick-cooking oatmeal rather than the instant stuff. They will revolutionize your perception of oatmeal. The amount of time it takes to prepare less-refined oatmeals is only a few minutes in the case of quick-cooking oatmeal and only fifteen to thirty minutes for the sturdier cuts. And it's cooking that hardly requires your attention; you can make oatmeal in a free moment and reheat it with a two-minute zap in the microwave.

What will make every bite worth savoring is the dried fruits' intensity amid the agreeable, buttery grains. In the words of our chef, "It's like adorning the plainest of black suits with an Hermès scarf. You need nothing else."

★ ★ ★

★ There's only one thing to remember: As with jewelry, you can overdo it. Be generous but not splashy.

This recipe, handed down for generations since Arthurian times, will provide two servings, one for tonight and one for tomorrow—or for whoever else must rise at this ungodly hour. Again, think of the recipe less as instructions and more as inspiration. The basic principle is simple: Use warmed milk to "cook" couscous and treat it like a princely porridge.

★ Reserve ½ cup milk and then combine all but the couscous, almonds, and cinnamon in a large saucepan. Bring the mixture to a simmer over low heat, but don't let it boil. Simmer for about 5 minutes, or until the fruit is plump. Remove the pan from the heat.

★ Stir in the couscous, cover the pan, and set it aside for 5 minutes. Meanwhile, microwave the reserved ½ cup of milk until it's very hot. Of course, you can also dirty another saucepan if it suits your fancy.

★ Mound the couscous in two bowls, sprinkle the "towers" with the almonds, dash some cinnamon on top, and pour half of the heated milk into each bowl, making a little moat around your couscous castle.

★ Dream of knights in shining armor or damsels in distress: your choice.

2½ cups milk

6 dried figs, stem end removed, and diced

4 dried apricots, sliced into thin strips

1 tablespoon currants, dried blueberries, cranberries, sour cherries, or other small dried fruit bits

1 tablespoon golden or dark raisins

1 tablespoon honey

Pinch of kosher salt

¾ cup couscous (the coarse, rapid-cooking type works best)

2 tablespoons toasted almonds, sliced or chopped coarsely

Big pinch of ground cinnamon

★

SERVES 2

1 large egg

¼ teaspoon vanilla extract

½ teaspoon grated lemon or
orange zest, optional

⅓ cup small-curd
cottage cheese

2 teaspoons vegetable oil

1½ tablespoons all-purpose
flour

⅛ teaspoon baking powder

Pinch of salt

Warm maple syrup, apple
butter, or preserves for
serving

Fresh berries, sliced banana,
toasted nuts, or sour cream
for serving, optional

★

MAKES 2 PANCAKES

Call them pancakes, griddle cakes, silver dollars, or anything you like, but our guess is that everyone delights in a stack of these breakfast rounds. Our father would make them most Sundays, ladling the batter into a hot skillet to delight us with crescent moons and stars, or rabbits and elephants—whatever shapes we'd request. How easily amused we were.

The lemon zest, cottage cheese, and vanilla that we've added here are hardly typical of the boxed pancake mix. These hot cakes are quick to prepare, easy to fry up, and light enough to feast on before running off to your spinning class or ironing your wrinkled skirt.

★ ★ ★

★ Place everything but the serving ingredients in a blender and whiz until smooth. Or mix by hand with a whisk.

★ Heat a nonstick skillet and brush the bottom surface lightly with oil. Pour the batter into the pan, forming 3- to 4-inch rounds. When bubbles appear on the batter's surface, flip the pancakes and brown the other side. (Don't be tempted to press the pancake with the spatula: let it puff up and fall slightly as it completes cooking. These are fluffy rather than leaden cakes.)

★ Serve with warmed maple syrup, apple butter, or preserves, along with fruits, nuts, or sour cream, if you like.

VARIATIONS

★ Ricotta cheese hot cakes are equally delicious, though a bit richer and more elegant. Substitute an equal amount of ricotta for the cottage cheese. Dust with confectioners' sugar.

★ If worries about elevated cholesterol torment your every waking hour, go back to bed. But here you can use 2 egg whites instead of the whole egg and substitute fat-free cottage cheese for the regular.

Good Morning Mush

Some farm cooks concoct mush from scratch each morning. They're up before dawn slopping the hogs and feeding the chickens, so time is obviously their friend. But this breakfast dish is actually as easy as pie. (Pie is actually not so easy.) You can keep a tray of this mush in your refrigerator (simply pour the extra mush into a lightly greased loaf pan) and saw off a piece or two at dawn, dust it with flour, and fry it with a bit of butter in less than a minute. Drench each bite in a puddle of warmed maple syrup and then head out to the fields.

(Oh yes, this is polenta, by the way. And yes, it is sold in a ready-to-cook log at the grocery, over by the egg substitutes and the fresh tortillas. No, the log does not taste anything like what you can cook up in a jiffy, and it costs ten times as much.)

Now, mush!

★ ★ ★

- ★ Bring the water and salt to a boil in a heavy saucepan.
- ★ Slowly stir in the cornmeal, using a whisk to keep lumps from forming.
- ★ Reduce the heat to low and, using a wooden spoon now, stir the mush occasionally as it simmers. After 10 minutes, the cornmeal will begin to thicken. Stir constantly for the next 10 minutes.
- ★ Serve the mush warm with milk, maple syrup, or honey.

4 cups water

Pinch of salt

1 cup yellow cornmeal

Milk, maple syrup, or honey for serving

★

SERVES 6

Great Day Granola

2½ cups quick-cooking oats

½ cup shredded
unsweetened coconut

½ cup sunflower seeds

1 cup pecan pieces

½ cup toasted wheat germ

2 tablespoons vegetable oil

¼ cup maple syrup

Pinch of salt

1 teaspoon vanilla extract

½ cup dried cranberries or
golden raisins

Yogurt, fresh fruit, or cereal
for serving

★

MAKES 5½ CUPS

Granola arrived, in all its earnestness, in the early 1970s, along with Szechwan cooking, baklava, Snapple, food processors, lite beer, salad bars, fettuccine Alfredo, and quiche. It was a big decade for the food industry.

There's nothing significantly healthy about granola. Oh sure, it's got lots of complex carbohydrates to propel you through a morning of errands, and it's crunchy, nutty, big, and bouncy—but the calories do tote along plenty of fat, particularly if you don't resist the coconut. Consumed in small quantities, however, granola can complement your morning yogurt. That's the granola complementing the yogurt, not the other way around.

★ ★ ★

★ Preheat the oven to 300°F.

★ Coat a 9 x 13-inch baking sheet with cooking spray.

★ In a large mixing bowl, toss the oats, coconut, sunflower seeds, pecans, and wheat germ together.

★ Combine the oil, maple syrup, and salt in a large glass measuring cup and heat in the microwave for 1 minute. Add the vanilla.

★ Pour the syrup mixture over the dry ingredients and toss to coat everything evenly.

★ Spread the mixture over the jelly-roll pan and bake for 40 minutes, stirring every 10 minutes.

★ Add the cranberries. Cool the mixture. Serve the granola on top of yogurt, fresh fruit, or your basic anemic breakfast cereal.

Dawn's Early Light

Whatever possessed you to agree to a seven o'clock flight when you live so far from the airport? Why is it, most mornings, you don't feel bright-eyed and bushy-tailed but slit-eyed and bushwacked? And the likelihood of hauling your butt out of bed another half hour earlier to make a sensible breakfast is about as likely as rising earlier to sort the buckets of nails in the garage into neatly labeled jars.

Regarding the importance of breakfast, studies show that starting a day with nothing in your stomach jeopardizes your ability to perform well, think clearly, maintain concentration, and act in a civil manner toward people who dare to get in your way. Almost a hundred years ago James Thurber's mother admonished her sons similarly regarding those newfangled automobiles: "Now don't you dare drive all over town without gasoline." She knew, and you know, that a complicated piece of machinery, like a car or a body, just can't get everywhere it needs to go without fuel. (Actually she was probably thinking about water for the radiator—but never mind. Water's important, too—in fact, studies show that eight glasses a day—)

So if you feel as though you can't possibly read the back of the Raisin Bran box one more time, it's time for a wake-up call. Harried fare needn't be horrible—though it often is. We've got heavenly cornmeal-and-cranberry biscuits for dunking in your cappuccino; a nifty nutty, no-bake trail bar; and even a refrigerator muffin mix to bake up in a mug that will be ready to head out the door even before you are. And for those whose tendency to oversleep is more the rule than the exception, we have even faster fare: Go-Power Bars and Rise 'n' Shiners breakfast cookies that are chock-full of carbs and protein for people on the go like you—like anyone you know is actually "on the stop"? Have a good day.

to make a sensible breakfast

Go-Power Bars

1 large egg

¼ cup packed light
brown sugar

1 tablespoon vegetable oil

½ teaspoon vanilla extract

¼ teaspoon grated nutmeg

¼ teaspoon ground
cardamon

¼ teaspoon ground ginger

Zest of 1 orange

¼ cup protein powder

2 tablespoons rice flour
or whole wheat flour

¼ teaspoon sea salt

½ cup old-fashioned
rolled oats

½ cup roasted soybeans

½ cup dried cranberries

½ cup walnuts, chopped

★

MAKES 6 BARS

Here is the ultimate get-up-and-go bar. While a lot of ingredients are summoned to the occasion, remember you'll be baking a week's worth of breakfasts in one fell swoop, and you're welcome to leave out some items and substitute others. That is, if you're orangeless, use lemons. If you're tired of raisins, add any dried fruit chopped into raisin-size bits. If you can't find the toasted soybeans, double the oatmeal or add the same amount of wheat germ to keep the high nutritional impact.

So go ahead, bake up a batch of these before your power breakfast tomorrow. Wake up with something to crow about.

★ ★ ★

★ Preheat the oven to 325°F. Line an 8 x 8-inch pan with foil and coat it with cooking spray.

★ Whisk together the egg, brown sugar, oil, vanilla extract, spices, and orange zest. Fold in the protein powder, rice or wheat flour, sea salt, oats, soybeans, cranberries, and walnuts to make a batter.

★ Scoop the mixture into the prepared pan and press it into an even layer with your fingers.

★ Bake for about 25 to 30 minutes; look for slightly toasted edges. Cool for 15 minutes, then invert the pan and peel off the foil.

★ Completely cool and cut the baked sheet into bars the size of your choosing. Wrap each bar in waxed paper, and seal. Maybe you can get the guy in the marketing department who knows Pagemaker to design you a little logo for the seal. And maybe a brand name with a fit-and-trim-and-upwardly-mobile ring to it, like "Germinator II" or "Outofmyways." And maybe you can even sell your breakfast bars in the breakroom because no one really wants to scarf down the doughnuts from yesterday's staff meeting. Let's say you sell ten a day, at two bucks each (that's a bargain! they're homemade for crying out loud!), and it only costs you . . . *wow!* it's not even 6 A.M., and look how much you've accomplished.

DAWN'S
EARLY LIGHT
187

1 cup honey or maple syrup

½ cup packed light brown
sugar

1½ cups peanut or another
nut butter, or tahini

1 cup nonfat dry milk powder

2 cups granola cereal (see
page 182 for our favorite)

½ cup sunflower seeds

½ cup sliced almonds

½ cup raisins, chocolate
chips, peanuts, dried sour
cherries, or dried cranberries
(pick one or make a
combination to fill
½ cup total)

★

MAKES 24 BARS

Not that you'll be trail-blazing at this hour of the morning, but since it's a jungle out there, we want you to be equipped. These dense, nutty bars have what it takes to get you through the morning, or at least to the office, where you can forage for other edible roots and berries.

★ Lightly oil a 9 x 13-inch baking pan. Line it with parchment or waxed paper, and lightly oil the top of the paper.

★ Combine the honey and sugar in a medium saucepan over medium-high heat. Stir to dissolve the sugar and then boil the mixture for 2 minutes.

★ Add the peanut butter and the powdered milk to the syrup and mix until it's well incorporated.

★ Add the cereal, seeds, nuts, and fruit. Stir to combine it all, and then press the mixture into the prepared pan. With a knife, score the outline of each bar—the size of the bar is your choice.

★ Refrigerate the mixture for 1 hour. Then finish cutting out the bars, wrapping each one individually in parchment, waxed paper, or cellophane. Store in cool place. The bars will keep for several weeks.

Breakfast Bickies

"Bickies" is Australian for cookies, while "cookies" is Australian for biscuits. And "biscuits" is—we got so confused we decided just to focus on this wonderfully hearty, grainy dipping biscotti (which is Italian for "biscotti") made of cornmeal, wheat germ, and protein powder. It's hardly sweet at all, making it our distinct favorite for dunking in breakfast tea or coffee. And for eating during the other daytime hours.

★ Preheat the oven to 350°F. Line a baking sheet with parchment paper.

★ In a large mixing bowl, combine the cornmeal, flour, protein powder, wheat germ, sugar, salt, and baking powder. Mix well.

★ Add the butter to the dry ingredients and pinch the mixture to make a coarse "meal," with no visible pieces of butter.

★ In a separate bowl, mix together the oil, eggs, and vanilla, and add this to the cornmeal mixture. Give it a few stirs and add the dried fruits. Mix thoroughly, and then divide the dough in half.

★ Press and roll the dough into two logs about 14 inches long each. Place the logs on the baking sheet and flatten them slightly.

★ Bake for 25 to 30 minutes. Cool for 7 minutes. Using a serrated knife, slice the logs into ½-inch slices; cut each biscotti carefully on the bias.

★ Turn down the oven temperature to 200°F. Return the cut cookies to the baking sheet and bake them for an additional 15 to 20 minutes, turning them once after 8 minutes. (Take care not to burn the cranberries.)

★ Once the cookies are cool, store them in an airtight container.

1⅓ cups white or yellow cornmeal

1 cup all-purpose flour

¼ cup protein powder

½ cup wheat germ

¼ cup sugar

¼ teaspoon salt

1 teaspoon baking powder

½ cup (1 stick) cold unsalted butter, cut into small pieces

¼ cup vegetable oil

2 large eggs

1 teaspoon vanilla extract

½ cup currants, soaked in warm water and drained

½ cup dried cranberries, soaked in warm water and drained

★

MAKES 30 BISCOTTI

½ cup (1 stick)
unsalted butter

½ cup packed light
brown sugar

1 egg

1 tablespoon grated
orange zest

2 tablespoons apple juice,
orange juice, or milk

1 cup whole wheat flour

1 teaspoon baking powder

1 teaspoon ground cinnamon

1 teaspoon ground ginger

½ cup barley nugget cereal
(such as Grape-Nuts)

2 tablespoons sesame seeds

2 tablespoons
sunflower seeds

½ cup currants or raisins

★

MAKES 18 TO 20 COOKIES

These breakfast cookies can be baked on a lazy Sunday, stored in packages of two in the freezer, and then defrosted the night before or microwaved as you hit the ground running. They're energy-rich and pretty darned wholesome, a welcome change from dry English muffins.

Here again, the dried fruit bits and nuts that you have on hand can be brought into play; just retain the general proportion of things, or you'll have something too dry to swallow or too gooey to eat in the car.

★ ★ ★

★ Preheat the oven to 350°F.

★ With a hand-mixer, cream the butter and sugar. Add the egg, zest, and juice, beating the mixture until fluffy.

★ In a separate bowl, blend together the flour, baking powder, cinnamon, and ginger. Add the cereal, sesame seeds, sunflower seeds, and currants.

★ Fold all the dry ingredients by hand into the mixing bowl to create the dough. Arrange spoonfuls 2 inches apart on an ungreased cookie sheet.

★ Bake for 10 to 12 minutes, until lightly golden.

★ Cool the cookies completely and store them in an airtight container.

Mug o' Muffin

This hearty batter can be prepared in ten minutes and then stowed for several days in the fridge. The idea is, you flip off the bedside alarm clock, stumble into the kitchen, turn on the oven, and pop in one or two mugs filled with muffin batter while you shower. And by the time you've dressed, rounded up your PDA, wallet, and glasses, a hot, fresh muffin is ready to accompany you out the door. And it's fiber-rich, which, as you know, is how all the ads and doctors want you to start your day.

★ ★ ★

★ Preheat the oven to 375°F.

★ In a large mixing bowl, whisk together the eggs and sugar. Add the melted butter, and finally add the coffee and the buttermilk. This should form a nice batter.

★ Fold all the dry ingredients into the egg batter, and add any optional items you'd like. This is the point at which the batter can hang out in a sealed plastic container or zippered bag in the refrigerator.

★ When you're ready to bake up a muffin, pour the batter into an oiled muffin pan or oven-proof coffee cup, filling each vessel three-quarters full. Bake for 20 to 25 minutes. (If you don't fill the muffin pan completely, pour some water into any empty cups to allow the tin to heat evenly.)

★ Either pop the muffin from the mug once it has cooled a bit, or take the mug along with a spoon to work.

2 large eggs

1 cup sugar

½ cup (1 stick) unsalted butter, melted

1 cup strong black coffee, cooled

2 cups buttermilk (or 2 cups milk with 2 tablespoons lemon juice stirred into it)

2½ cups all-purpose flour or whole wheat pastry flour (or 1¼ cups all-purpose flour and 1¼ cups whole wheat flour)

2½ teaspoons baking soda

3 cups high-fiber bran cereal, such as All-Bran or Bran Buds

3 tablespoons poppy seeds, optional

½ cup chopped nuts, optional

½ cup plumped dried fruit, such as golden raisins, sour cherries, cranberries, optional

★

MAKES 20 LARGE MUFFINS (HOW BIG IS YOUR MUG?)

Index

Agua Fresca de Cantalupo, 98
Agua Fresca de Melon Dulce, 99
Agua Fresca de Pepino, 99
Agua Fresca de Sandia, 99
All Dal-ed Up, 150
Almonds, Chocolate, 34
Animal Crackers in My Goop, 81
Anisette and Mint, Macerated Melons with, 80
Apples
  Campfire Apples, 54
  Huntsman Cheese and Apples, 142
  Vermont Golden Apple Snow, 103
Apricots, 107. See also Fruit, dried
  Apricot Blizzard, 105
Avocado Mask and Dip, 122

Balsamic Dip, Garlic, 152
Bananas, 107
  Banana Ice Cream, 106
  Banana Strawberry Sorbet, 105
Bedtime Blini, 66–67
Berries, 107. See also specific kinds
  Just a Trifle, 81
  Oats and Berries, 81
Beverages. 13, 172. See also Cocktails
  agua frescas, 98–99
  beauty treatments and, 121, 123
  hot drinks, 18–19, 48–53
  ice cream sodas, 5
  lassis, 126–27
  smoothies, 125, 169–71
  lemonades & limeades, 97
Biscotti, Chicken-Liver, 40–41
Black Pepper Citronette, 133
Blini, Bedtime, 66–67
Blond Hot Chocolate, 48
Blue Cheese Vinaigrette, 133
Bread. See Toasts
Breakfast Bickies, 189
Brewed Cider, 51
Buckeye Bars, 8
Buffalo Wingnuts, 116

Cake, Chocolate Sour Cherry, 70–71
Campfire Apples, 54
Candies, 32–35, 43–44, 112–13
Cantaloupe. See Melons
Cat food, 42
Catnip Nips, 42
Cereal, 178, 181–82
  Buffalo Wingnuts, 116
  Mug o' Muffin, 191
  No-Bake Trail Bars, 188
  Shaggy Dogs, 56–57
  South of the Border Mix-Up, 115
Checkered Mixes, 114–17
Cheese. See also Parmesan
  Brie Fondue for One, 118
  Huntsman Cheese and Apples, 142
  Plowman's Toast, 141
  Welsh Not-So-Rarebit, 119
Cherries
  Chocolate Cherry Jubilee, 170
  Chocolate Sour Cherry Cake, 70–71
Cherry Cola, 5
Chicken-Liver Biscotti, 40–41
Chickpeas
  Gonzo Garbanzos, 111
Chocolate, 33
  Blond Hot Chocolate, 48
  Buckeye Bars, 8
  Chocolat Chaud, 49
  Chocolate Almonds, 34
  Chocolate Cherry Jubilee, 170
  Chocolate-Night Martini, 30
  Chocolate Sour Cherry Cake, 70–71
  Cocoa-Nutter Butter, 170
  Frosted Chocolate Mint Leaves, 35
  Ice-Cream Bites in Chocolate Shells, 31
  Macaroon Sandwich Cookies, 68–69
  Mints for Your Pillow, 43–44
  Mocha Java Jolt, 169
  Shaggy Dogs, 56–57
  White Chocolate Bark, 32–33
Chopped Ice Cream, 22–23
Cider, Brewed, 51

Clamato juice
  Shoot the Moon, 60
Classic Vinaigrette, 133
Cocktails, 30, 60, 97
Cocoa-Nutter Butter, 170
Coconut
  Macaroon Sandwich Cookies, 68–69
Coffees, 40
Congee, 17
Congestion Buster, 18
Cookies & bars, 8–9, 26, 68–69, 186–90
Cornmeal
  Breakfast Bickies, 189
  Good Morning Mush, 181
  Polenta Crackers, 91
Cottage Cheese Hot Cakes, 180
Couscous Castle with a Milk Moat, 179
Crackers, 38, 86–87, 91
Crème fraîche, 163
Crisped Salami Chips, 88
Crispy Potato Spoons, 89
Croutons, Goat-Cheese, 100
Cuatro Aguas Fresca, 98–99
Cucumbers
  Agua Fresca de Pepino, 99
  Cucumber Slurry, 153
  English Cucumber Facial and Frappé, 123
Cures-What-Ails-Ya Soup, 12

Daily Salad in a Newspaper Cone, 160–61
Desserts, 72–73, 81–83, 103, 165. See also Cake; Cookies & bars; Ice cream; Pudding
Dips & spreads, 118–19, 122, 135, 150–55
Dog food, 40–41
Don't-Be-So-Stuffy Soup, 14–15
Double-Down Doughnuts, 143
Doughnuts, Double-Down, 143

Easy Pecan-ese Mix, 117
Eggs
  Egg Roll-Ups, 78–79
  Everyday Egg Roll-Ups, 78

Maki-Style Omelets with Nori or Herbs, 79
Slow-Cooked, Soft-Scrambled Eggs, 62–63
Son-in-Law's Eggs, 174
Tofu-ed Eggs, 63
English Cucumber Facial and Frappé, 123
Everyday Egg Roll-Ups, 78
Everything's Coming Up Tuscan Mix, 114

Far-Flung Turkey Hash, 64–65
Figgy Toasts, 144
Fire-Roasted Taters, 46, 55
Flambé the Night Away, 165
Fondue for One, 118
Four Energizers, 168–70
Freezer Pleezers, 104–7
Frosted Chocolate Mint Leaves, 35
Fruits, 107. *See also specific kinds*
dried, 71
    Couscous Castle with a Milk Moat, 179
    Easy Pecan-ese Mix, 117
    Jeweled Gruel, 178
    White Chocolate Bark, 32–33
Flambé the Night Away, 165
Fruit Salsa, 93
Grandma's Old-Fashioned Trifle, 81
Green Tea-for-Two Smoothie, 125
The Pavlova Variations, 72–73
Quick Fruit Sauce, 25
Wonton Skinnies, 162

Garlic Balsamic Dip, 152
Get-Well-Sooner Pudding, 13
Ginger
Gingery Lemon Infusion, 19
Honeydew and Ginger Lassi, 127
Snappy Ginger Snaps, 26
Ginseng Sling, 169
Goat Cheese
Goat-Cheese Croutons, 100
Visions of Chèvre Plums, 83
Gonzo Garbanzos, 111
Good Morning Mush, 181
Go-Power Bars, 186–87
Graham crackers
Buckeye Bars, 8
Gram's Cracker Bars, 9
Gram's Cracker Bars, 9
Grandma's Old-Fashioned Trifle, 81
Grapes, 107
White Grape Sorbet, 104
Great Day Granola, 182
Green Tea-for-Two Smoothie, 125

Green Tea Gazpacho, 102
Grits, Quick Greasy-Spooner, 173

Have a Cow, 5
Hoisin Drizzle, 135
Homemade Ice Cream Sandwiches, 24–25
Honey
Honeyed Orange Dipping Sauce, 135
Pistachio and Honey Lassi, 127
Honeydew melon. *See* Melons
Hot and Sweet Pumpkin-Seed Brittle, 112–13
Huntsman Cheese and Apples, 142

Ice Cream
Banana Ice Cream, 106
Cherry Cola, 5
Chopped Ice Cream, 22–23
Flambé the Night Away, 165
Grandma's Old-Fashioned Trifle, 81
Have a Cow, 5
Ice-Cream Bites in Chocolate Shells, 31
Ice Cream Sandwich Waffles, 25
Orange Creamsicle, 5
Raspberry Ice Cream, 106
Snappy Ice Cream Sandwiches, 24
Tropical Tower, 81
Impromtu Pizza, 2–3
Indian Spice Lassi, 127

Japanese Sake Bath, 120
Jeweled Gruel, 178
Just a Trifle, 81

Lemons & lemon juice
Congestion Buster, 18
Gingery Lemon Infusion, 19
Lemon Lassi, 127
Pink Lemonade, 97
State-Fair Lemon Shake-Ups, 96–97
Tomcat Collins, 97
Lentils
All Dal-ed Up, 150
Limes & lime juice
Limeade, 97
Tangy Lime Dipping Sauce, 135
Liver-, Chicken, Biscotti, 40–41
Lots of Lassis, 126–27

Macaroon Sandwich Cookies, 68–69
Macerated Melons with Anisette and Mint, 80
Maki-Style Omelets with Nori or Herbs, 79

Marshmallows
Marshmallow Sauce, 27
Shaggy Dogs, 56–57
Mascarpone Cheese and Plums, Spiced, 142
Mashed Potato Pancakes, 4
Melons, 107
Agua Fresca de Cantalupo, 98
Agua Fresca de Melon Dulce, 99
Agua Fresca de Sandia, 99
Honeydew and Ginger Lassi, 127
Macerated Melons with Anisette and Mint, 80
Microwave Risotto, 77
Middle-of-the-Night Miso Soup, 128–29
Milk, 15
Don't-Be-So-Stuffy Soup, 14–15
Milk Toast, 16
Mint
Frosted Chocolate Mint Leaves, 35
Macerated Melons with Anisette and Mint, 80
Mint or Persian Lassi, 127
Mints for Your Pillow, 43–44
Miso Soup, Middle-of-the-Night, 128–29
Mocha Java Jolt, 169
Muffin, Mug o', 191
Mug o' Muffin, 191

Nectarine Tarts, Sourdough, 142
Nighttime Chai, 52–53
Nighttime Salade Niçoise Lettuce Cups, 132–33
No-Bake Trail Bars, 188
Nut Butter
Cocoa-Nutter Butter, 170
Nuts. *See also specific kinds*
Everything's Coming Up Tuscan Mix, 114
Gram's Cracker Bars, 9
South of the Border Mix-Up, 115
Nutty Tofu Spread, 151

Oatmeal
Jeweled Gruel, 178
Oats
Go-Power Bars, 186–87
Great Day Granola, 182
Oats and Berries, 81
Oranges & orange juice
Honeyed Orange Dipping Sauce, 135
Orange Creamsicle, 5
Oysters
Shoot the Moon, 60

Pancakes, 4, 6–7, 66–67, 180
Papayas, 107
  Papaya Pick-Me-Up-and-Put-Me-Down, 172
Parmesan cheese
  Parmesan Popcorn, 110
  Parmesan Shortbread, 38
  Parmesan Wafers, 86–87
The Pavlova Variations, 72–73
Peaches, 107
  Peachy-Keen Gazpacho, 101
Peanut butter
  Buckeye Bars, 8
  Nutty Tofu Spread, 151
Peanuts
  Buffalo Wingnuts, 116
Pears
  Plowman's Toast, 141
Pecans
  Easy Pecan-ese Mix, 117
  Twice-Spiced Pecans, 117
Pet food, 40–42
Pineapples, 107
  Pineapple Rum Sorbet, 105
Pink Lemonade, 97
Pistachios
  Pistachio and Honey Lassi, 127
  White Chocolate Bark, 32–33
Pizza, Impromtu, 2–3
Plowman's Toast, 141
Plums, 107
  Spiced Mascarpone Cheese and Plums, 142
  Visions of Chèvre Plums, 83
Polenta, 61, 181
  Polenta Crackers, 91
Popcorn, Parmesan, 110
Popover Pancakes, 6–7
Potatoes
  Crispy Potato Spoons, 89
  Fire-Roasted Taters, 55
  Mashed Potato Pancakes, 4
Pudding, Get-Well-Sooner, 13
Pumpkin Punch, 171
Pumpkin seeds
  Easy Pecan-ese Mix, 117
  Hot and Sweet Pumpkin-Seed Brittle, 112–13

Quick Fruit Sauce, 26
Quick Greasy-Spooner Grits, 173

Raspberry Ice Cream, 106
Rice
  Congee, 17
  Get-Well-Sooner Pudding, 13
  Microwave Risotto, 77
  Rice Water Tonic, 13
  Risotto 'Round Midnight Cakes, 76
Rice Paper Rolls, 134–35
Rise 'n' Shiners, 190
Rum Sorbet, Pineapple, 105

Sake Bath, Japanese, 120
Salad dressings, 133
Salads, 132–33, 160–61
Salami Chips, Crisped, 88
Salmon, Smoked, Wedges, 158–59
Salsa, Fruit , 93
Sauces, 26–27. *See also* Dips & Spreads; Salsa
Shaggy Dogs, 56–57
Shiitake mushrooms, 154
  Shiitake Paté, 154–55
Shoot the Moon, 60
Shrimp
  Polenta with Scampi, 61
Simple Tomato Gazpachos with Goat-Cheese Croutons, 100
Slow-Cooked, Soft-Scrambled Eggs, 62–63
Smoked Salmon Wedges, 158–59
Smooshed Tomato Toasts, 140
Snappy Ginger Snaps, 26
Snappy Ice Cream Sandwiches, 24
Son-in-Law's Eggs, 174
Sorbets, 104–5
Soups, 12, 14–15, 17, 100–2, 128–29
Sourdough Nectarine Tarts, 142
South of the Border Mix-Up, 115
Spiced Mascarpone Cheese and Plums, 142
State-Fair Lemon Shake-Ups, 96–97
Strawberry Sorbet, Banana, 105
Stuffing
  Don't-Be-So-Stuffy Soup, 14–15
Sugar Crisps with Fruit Salsa, 92–93
Sugared Raisin Bread Crisps, 39
Sweet potatoes
  Far-Flung Turkey Hash, 64–65
  Sweet Potato Oven Fries, 90

Tangy Lime Dipping Sauce, 135
Teas, 19, 52–53
  green, 125

Green Tea-for-Two Smoothie, 125
Green Tea Gazpacho, 102
Three Facial Frappés, 121–23
Tiramisu Tower, 82
Toasts, 16, 39, 136–37, 140–44
Tofu
  Nutty Tofu Spread, 151
  Shiitake Paté, 154–55
  Tofu-ed Eggs, 63
Tomatoes
  Simple Tomato Gazpachos with Goat Cheese Croutons, 100
  Smooshed Tomato Toasts, 140
Tomcat Collins, 97
Tossing and Turnovers, 136–37
Tropical Mask and Milkshake, 121
Tropical Tower, 81
Tuna
  Nighttime Salade Niçoise Lettuce Cups, 132–33
Turkey Hash, Far-Flung, 64–65
Turnovers, Tossing and, 136–37
Twice-Spiced Pecans, 117
Two Vanilla Coffees, 50

Vanilla
  Vanilla Iced Coffee, 50
  Vanilla Latte, 50
Vermont Golden Apple Snow, 103
Vodka
  Chocolate-Night Martini, 30
  Shoot the Moon, 60
  Tomcat Collins, 97

Waffles, Ice Cream Sandwich, 25
Wanton Wontons, 162–64
Watermelon. *See* Melons
Welsh Not-So-Rarebit, 119
White Chocolate Bark, 32–33
White Grape Sorbet, 104
Wontons, 162–64
Wraps, 132–35

Yogurt
  frozen
    Mocha Java Jolt, 169
    Pumpkin Punch, 171
  lassis, 127
  Tropical Mask and Milkshake, 121

Zesty Wonton Triangles, 164

About the Authors

Michael J. Rosen is the author, editor, and illustrator of a wide variety of some forty books, including works for both adults and children. Much of his efforts involve philanthropic volumes to benefit Share Our Strength's fight against hunger, including the children's books *The Greatest Table* and *Food Fight*. He is also the editor of the biennial *Mirth of a Nation: The Best Contemporary Humor* and several philanthropic anthologies, such as *Horse People* and *Dog People,* that aid animal welfare agencies across the nation. His illustrations have appeared in *Gourmet, The New Yorker*, and in several of his books for young readers. He lives in central Ohio, where he served as literary director at The Thurber House for twenty years.

Sharon Reiss has worked in the food industry for twenty-two years. She operated a catering company, Cornucopia, for ten of those years. For six years, she served as an executive chef and event planner. Now a food consultant, food stylist, and recipe developer, Sharon's has a client list that includes Robert Rothschild's Farm, The Wilton Company, Cheryl's Cookies, and Smithfield Hams. Her cookbooks include *Cooking from the Pantry*, for the Longaberger Company, and two that are designed and written by Amy and David Butler: *Lip-Smacking Jams and Jellies* and *Farmhands' Favorite Pies*. She lives in Columbus, Ohio.